In Your
DARKEST HOUR:
Hope For the Hopeless, Broken, and Suicidal

By MICHELE D. ALUOCH

PRESS

Table of Contents

Preface

Michele D. Aluoch is the owner and director of River of Life Professional Counseling LLC. As a Licensed Professional Clinical Counselor (LPCC) Michele is credentialed at the highest level of counseling licensure in Ohio. Since receiving this licensure in 1998 she has demonstrated a passion for seeing the lives of individuals, families, couples, and groups changed and hope restored. She offers outpatient clinical counseling to diagnose and treat emotional and mental disorders. She also provides psychoeducational seminars and groups to persons in the community, schools, teachers, churches and businesses on a variety of emotional healing topics.

Prior to this book Michele has authored the "Counseling Corner" newsletter and the book "Sanctuary: A Shelter For Your Soul" with here and now biblically based meditations for overcoming stress, depression, and anxiety. Michele has been a provider of ongoing continuing education courses since 2008 which are pre-approved by the State of Ohio Counselor, Social Worker, and Marriage and Family Therapist Board toward state continuing education requirements for professional counselors, professional clinical counselors and supervising counselors in the state of

Ohio. In addition to River of Life Professional Counseling LLC, Michele works as a Care Coordination Specialist at Dublin Springs Hospital in Dublin, Ohio. She is an active seminar designer and presenter for their educational series.

Michele not only is a clinical counselor but is also an ordained nondenominational Christian minister who ministers nationally and internationally. Since 1995 she has taught religious education classes at all grade levels from preschool through adulthood. As such, she teaches practical, relevant, and age appropriate applications on spiritual implications of real life issues. Her dedication and sensitive examples have resonated with people of diverse cultures and groups nationally and internationally. Michele's ministry style implores a genuine concern and sincerity for connecting hurting people with practical suggestions and solutions. She also ministers through prayer, singing and playing worship music, preaching, and teaching as an itinerant minister. In 2008 she founded Call to Holiness International Ministry in Columbus, Ohio. Currently, she assists in equipping and mentoring people in both secular and church settings towards achieving emotional and spiritual wellness through applying Christian Biblical principles in their lives.

Author's Note

This book is for those of you who feel sad, hurt, depressed, anxious, and ready to give up hope. This book is for those of you who feel like too many layers of life have piled up. It offers inspiration and perspective, hope, challenges, and practical alternatives. It incorporates clinical counseling principles as well as Bible examples and principles.

However, this book is not a quick and easy replacement for those who need face to face clinical counseling treatment for mental health issues. In addition, this book is in no way designed to replace or substitute for what a personal and intimate relationship with Jesus Christ and personal prayer, Bible study, and other disciplines of a Christian life may give.

Most of all this book provides perspective on what it is that keeps a person down and stuck. It relies on the premise that there are alternatives and choices both naturally and spiritually in a relationship which facilitate movement away from feeling stuck to a truly abundant life. This book directly responds to the questions:

- What if you could think differently about things?

- What if you could choose more positive behaviors?
- What if you could expect God's best?
- What if today could be your resurrection day of hope, healing, restoration, clarity, strength?
- You will begin to grasp little by little that a life not riddled with pain at every turn is possible. I believe with you through prayer that by the time you end reading this book the Lord God Himself will have begun a marvellous new work in you and you will have taken some steps on the road to freedom. What feels like your darkest hour does not have to mean doom and despair. It can be the catalyst for a new improved direction. There is strength and hope beyond you. All is not lost. Let's believe and study together how this change and transformation even in the darkest hour is possible- even for you.

I celebrate with you in advance everything God desires to do in and through your life. May you through this book come to a greater understanding of the reality that your life is not in vain. There is only one of you which God ever will create. He smiled and said you were "very good" when He created you. He was well pleased. Genesis 1:31 states, "And God saw everything that he had made, and, behold, it was very good. And the evening and the morning were the sixth day."

It is still possible for all He purposed in your life to unfold. May you have an ear to hear and eyes to see and perceive what the Lord sees is possible in you.

Believing all is possible in and by His strength in your life,

Michele Aluoch

Dedication

This book is dedicated to any of you who has battled hopelessness, discouragement, brokenness, grief, or stress. There comes a point at which you have probably asked, "how much more can I take?" This book is for those of you who are struggling to find hope, searching for meaning in the mess, and desiring a more fulfilling life than the present that I've written this book.

This book is for you if:

- you feel alone and abandoned
- you believe you are misunderstood by others
- you are ailing in a hospital bed
- you are struggling through day to day tasks
- your life and the people, places, and things in it no longer make sense
- you are experiencing grief and stress
- you have considered giving up
- you wonder if anyone anywhere even cares about you
- you are searching for meaning
- I want you to know that you are not alone in those feelings. You are not alone in the questioning and

trying to make sense of things. You are not alone in the wondering, "what next?" If you are stuck in the place of your darkest hour and it is hard to find the dawn, this book is dedicated to you. If you need empathy, understanding, and perspective, this book is for you. Finally, if you need some practical direction to take steps from the darkest hour to a better place this book is for you.

My hope and sincere prayer is that as we embark on this journey through the pages of this book that your life will become a testimony of real positive change and ability as well as God's strength beyond yourself. You don't have to stay in the darkest hour because it is painful, disabling or familiar. May your mind begin to conceive of healthy possibilities and your actions begin to yearn for the life giving choices which will allow you to live an abundant and fulfilling life out from under the cover of the darkest hour.

Acknowledgements

I would like to thank God for allowing all the oppor-tunities He has seen come through my life. Only by having gone through the years of life circumstances I have endured and faced by His grace have I been able to develop some skills which have kept me going thus far. I thank God not only for every enjoyable moment He has allowed in my life but also for the painful, troublesome darkest hour moments because it was and is in those I continue to be shaped beyond myself. When there have been more questions than answers God has always been there. When troubles seem to keep coming God was there. When people behaved anything but kind gentle and lovely God was there. When tears, questions, and uncertainty seemed like regular occurrences God was still there behind the scenes in ways of which I am unaware.

I believe it is for this reason that the clients whose paths I've crossed in counseling, those I've been also to minster to, and lay persons who I've interacted with have been able to state, "you sound like you really understand what I've gone through." I've learned that our circum-stances, especially the painful ones aren't just for us but also for some other people who may someday cross our paths. I have been blessed by how my darkest hours are a means for understanding and empathizing with the darkest hours in others' lives. 2 Corinthinas1:3-7 has proven true:

> Blessed be God, even the Father of our Lord Jesus Christ, the Father of mercies, and the God of all comfort; Who comforts us in all our tribulation, that we may be able to comfort them which are in any trouble, by the comfort wherewith we ourselves are comforted of God. And whether we be afflicted, it is for your consolation and salvation, which is effectual in the enduring of the same sufferings which we also suffer: or whether we be comforted, it is for your consolation and salvation.

At present there are still places in my life that feel painful and may seem uncertain but they are nonetheless training grounds for victory and new hope to come forth in time.

I also thank every client throughout my training and practice as a clinical counselor who has allowed me to journey with him or her through their situations. It takes great vulnerability and humility to allow a new person, especially an outsider, to journey with you into those painful places. I am appreciative of those times of hearing the stories of so many different circumstances of hurt and pain with sincerity and honest vulnerability. I am also grateful for the willingness of clients to stick with me through the journey to the other side of their story until we could see new beliefs and behaviors and lay hold of new hope and possibility in life.

I thank every church and ministry nationally and internationally which has allowed me the opportunity to grow my faith through witnessing the diverse needs of people in various cultures. I thank my mentors and pastors through the years for allowing me venues to teach, preach, disciple, and hold groups, retreats and seminars. Through these experiences I have been able to learn that although the needs of people many manifest differently at the core people in different cultures and facing different issues are all facing the same central issue- the search for value and meaning in life, something beyond themselves which makes the journey worth enduring.

Thanks to my parents, grandparents, and family from childhood on who raised me modeling faith and endurance in tough times. I saw the value of perseverance and hard work, humility, and trust in God even though the storms of life.

Thanks to the countless people who may be in their darkest hour now but who continue to search ad seek, ask difficult questions and not give up. Your perseverance keeps me going too.

Thanks to those who did not even know the implications of the hurt and pain, mistreatment, and wounds in our lives for they make all of us seek something better. It is only by experiencing the counterfeit that we can recognize and fully appreciate the genuine blessing when it comes.

Thanks to friends, colleagues, and co laborers in Christ who encouraged me to keep writing and speaking when my own circumstances were being shaken. Thanks for seeing the other side of the darkest hour for me and offering words of hope, affirmation ad support.

To all of you who have endured with me through the hours of work, writing, research, and revisions of this book and other emotional healing outreach I offer my deepest of gratitude. I trust that because of the roles you have played in my life's journey many more will be blessed through this book. God bless you all.

Do You Want To Be Healed?

The question "do you want to be healed?" may sound like a rather foolish one at first being that one might assume that you would not have sought out help, a counselor, a friend, a minister, Scriptures, doctors, or other assistance if you did not want change. Right? However, the fact is that there are many reasons you may be seeking help now. Often there is sheer frustration of being in the same struggles for what feels like too long. A second reason you may seek help is that you are curious about options. The question "what can you do for me?" is all too common as it is part of the human condition for us to wonder what even experts or professionals could do to make a difference when the pains of life abound. Thirdly, you may simply want acknowledgement and validation for your personal journey. You might eve think that if things don't get better at least you will wear the issue like a badge or identifier. Or example, you may say, "I am a person in pain. I am an abuse victim. I am an alcoholic. I am a troubled person. I am anxious and depressed. I am at my wits end." The problem with this is that while there is always a story behind each one of our lives only we can decide if the story of the troubles and issues of our lives will determine who we are from here.

Let me be clear about this distinction. You have a choice. You may not have had a choice about some of the awful things that have beset you thus far. As you enter into the next chapter of your life, on the other hand, you have a choice about what you will do about issues years later.

This is where the last and final group of you comes in. This book is for you. You may have been through things in life that have pulled you down, weighed on your heart, tested and tried your hope, or made you feel like giving up. Yet in the depth of your soul you believe there is some help and healing somewhere. "There has to be something better than this" is your motto. You want to get well but have hurt for so long that you have found it difficult to conceptualize what being well would be or how you could get there. For you there is hope and encouragement, truth and reality, newness and hope.

You are not alone. There is a story in the Bible of a place called Bethesda which had a pool where the sick and invalids would come to be healed. There may be a story of your life too of where you and others plagued with hurts and pains have come prior to trying this pool. It may be the countless doctor's offices, hospitals, relationships, drugs, habits, and options you have tried.

There are some key principles in the Bible story in John 5:1-9 that may help your situation today. Let's start by reading the story first.

After this there was a feast of the Jews; and Jesus went up to Jerusalem. Now there is at Jerusalem by the sheep market a pool, which is called in the Hebrew tongue Bethesda, having five porches. In these lay a great multitude of impotent folk, of blind, halt, withered, waiting for the moving of the water. For an angel went down at a certain season into the pool, and troubled the water: whosoever then first after the troubling of the water stepped in was made whole of whatsoever disease he had. And a certain man was there, which had an infirmity thirty and eight years. When Jesus saw him lie, and knew that he had been now a long time in that case, he saith unto him, Wilt thou be made whole? The impotent man answered him, Sir, I have no man, when the water is troubled, to put me into the pool: but while I am coming, another steppeth down before me. Jesus saith unto him, Rise, take up thy bed, and walk. And immediately the man was made whole, and took up his bed, and walked: and on the same day was the sabbath.

The first thing that stands out about this story is that it says there "lay a great multitude of impotent folk, of blind, lame, and withered." There is a place you get used to when you have felt stuck for years. In particular we read about one man who was an invalid for thirty eight years. Imagine this. This mean that literally half of his lifespan was robbed by immobility. He watched other blind, immobile, hurting people get healed but he stayed lying there. He stayed on a mat for thirty eight ears watching people go in and pool bound and coming out healed and whole.

It could have been an encouragement when "a great number of people" were changed when the water was stirred. This man could have considered told also that he could also be part of this great number. He could have imagined walking, jumping, and getting around parts of the town he hadn't seen in years! But then he would have had to choose that. It would be much more natural and far more tempting to think like me and you do at times, "I can't imagine better for me. I see those others have newness and wholeness in their lives but not me."

When Jesus asked him specifically, "what is holding you up? What is keeping you back?," the man stated that no one would take him to the pool. Maybe he was like you are- waiting for some social supports to be there to listen to your story and help you out. Maybe he is like you waiting for a specific something to tell you it is okay for you to believe for better than how it has been.

The key though is noticing Jesus' reaction. He did not physically put the man in the water. He did not carry him himself. The man thought he needed someone to carry him and place him in the water. Jesus told him to go to the water. Essentially this is saying "do you have faith to believe that when you get to the water something will happen for you like others?" Until we all answer this question we will never be ready to move from our stuck place.

It is important to know the history of this pool of Bethesda. When people got into this pool who had diseases and troubles, angels of the Lord would stir the water and the sick would be made well. The point is they had to get to the water and get inside it for something to happen. In the Bible the water represents the presence of God and His ability in spite of our utter despair, weakness, and sense of wanting to give up. Through reading this book you will discover what some of the hindrances are that have kept you from getting into and receiving what the water of God's presence and strength has for your life. You will learn that you have choices and alternatives to what has kept you stuck and in despair.

The word *Bethesda* means house of mercy. Maybe you have experienced so much disdain and shunning from people because of the sores on your body and heart. Maybe you have judged yourself and your life. However, when you come to the water where the angel of the Lord, His very presence- Jesus Himself, stands with you- mercy comes. Mercy is tied to God's unmerited favor or grace for you. He wants you well not because you did it all right in life, not because you or I deserve it, but because the God of the universe has mercy on us. Notice the man got well once he picked up His mat. He immediately got well when he stopped believing the lie that he'd be an invalid the thirty ninth and fortieth years! He did not even physically get into the water of the pool. Once Jesus, who is the person of the Living Water in the Bible, boldly and authoritatively spoke to him with a new belief the healing water was activated in his life.

The process of healing and wholeness begins with one question- "do you want to be made well?" Think about this for a while. Do not rush your answer. Perhaps you don't even have a concept of what "well" would look like. Do you want to believe that things can and will be better than they have been- not necessarily problem free but that there is a place of grace, peace, strength, healing and wholeness? If you think you would like to find alternatives to the dark, stuck feelings which you have lived in lately, consider journeying with me to see how God's strength is made perfect in the weakness and most frail and fragile and hopeless of all situations- your situation.

"Do you have faith to believe that when you get to the water something will happen for you like others?" Until we all answer this question we will never be ready to move from our stuck place.

<u>Prayer</u>:

God, we are weak but we know that deep down we want something different then the hurt, pain, despair, hopelessness, immobility, paralysis of heart, soul, and body we have lived in. We have come to our own point of impossibility. We can't conceive how to get into the water. We have seen others get hope at times but we wonder if that pool of healing and hope is for us? Forgive our doubt. Assist us as we take our mats, our excuses, our rationales out from under us and listen to your command to walk into the pool. Help us as we don't know where the pool will take us. Painful things have at least become certain things for us. The pools of your rescue are new and scary. If you but will say to us that you believe we can carry the mats to the water and walk in we shall obey today ad go in. Take our weak hearts, our feeble bodies our broken lives. Only you can stir the waters. Only you can bring life where death, discouragement, and stuck feelings abound. Whether it be months, years, or decades we believe that just as many were healed by this pool "many" can include us. Begin by touching our beliefs as we walk into the pool. Touch our bodies. Touch our lives that we can accept the reality of your healing and wholeness that we have come to deny and rule out. We answer "yes" to your question-"yes", we want to be made whole? We have tried it ourselves. We now give you permission to make and remake us. Make us whole. In Jesus' name we pray. Amen.

The Roadmap To Discouragement

If you have gone through many stressors in life you may feel a sense of what is called de-realization- like what you are going through is so pressuresome and over-whelming that it cannot possibly be happening to you. You may feel like you are watching a movie about someone else's life from a distance. There is shock and a thought that "I can't believe this all happened to me." In addition to shock you may also feel grief, sadness, anger, ques-tioning, confusion, injustice, and a host of other emotions as you try to make sense of what does not feel rational, fair, or just.

Over time layers piled up to get to where you are now. As a result, it may take some time for the layers to be undone. Throughout this book you may find some critical factors which may assist you in discovering and coping with various components of the hopeless and helpless feelings you are going through.

Counselors tend to describe the layers using the analogy of peeling an onion. All the layers of your life's stuff seem to come together into what right now may feel like one big ball of mess. Sometimes when layers of stress come one after another there is barely time to deal with each layer as it hits. The layers weave together layer upon layer into this onion. Only by peeling the layers of your onion delicately and slowly away can you deal with each in a sensitive timing individualized to your personal healing process.

Regardless of what issues or how many layers make up your particular onion I find that there are no two more important parts of a person that contribute to who and what he or she becomes than his or her: 1) thoughts and 2) words. What a person believes or his thoughts show where he stands on an issue. This is where his heart really is on something. First you and I will explore how beliefs are the foundations for actions and reactions. If you think negatively, your actions will likely keep you hurt, oppressed, and feeling victimized. Next, we will look at the words or what one confesses about or over a situation. We will see how words are catalysts to initiate actions.

What I Believe

Maybe you like so many others have argued that what happened to you made you stressed out, depressed, or hopeless. However, this rationale cannot be the entire truth because some of the people who go through the seemingly worst situations in life are able to keep going on with hope in what would seem hopeless. Why do some find courage in the oddest places? Why do some muster up inner resources and deal with life with resiliency and flexibility that few others have?

It all starts with beliefs. If you believe that your life is hopeless, helpless, and it is all over then you will begin to live that way. Even if something good is around the bend you will likely overlook it. If you believe that bad things always happen to you then you may assume that the next thing is always bad. Even if God wants to show Himself as the grace filled, kind, loving, personal God who wants to do a miracle you may not be willing to receive it because you are used to having a stuck mindset.

The Bible in Romans 8:28 tells us that "we know that all things work together for good to them that love God, to them who are the called according to his purpose." (Romans 8:28) But what if you don't believe deep down that anyone, even God could love you? Then even though God does love you and wants the best in your life you will refuse to see it.

Wouldn't it be an awful thing for God to want to provide a new and healthy sense of perspective on a situation that seems beyond repair but you or I insist on remaining bound? That's exactly what happens when you hold on to a belief that is self defeating. As a result you get locked into the pain to where it is all you see. The negative belief telling one unpleasant side of the story may actually seem realistic if you are hurt and pained enough.

Think of someone who lives with chronic physical pain, for example. The pain is real to where it aches to move one's joints or walk up and down stairs. What if in the middle of that pain God could provide a healthy sense of perspective on things? For example, what if He could give a perspective on learning how to eat healthy, take nutritional supplements, or enhance mobility and exercise the very joints which otherwise would atrophy? What if God could help take the focus from magnifying the pain to magnifying the possibilities and expectations?

There are numerous examples of people who could have given up but chose alternative beliefs. For example, Nick Vujicic was born with no arms, a torso and a few pods with one toe on each for feet. Instead of His parents who were Christians succumbing to the belief that God forsook them, they saw this unique child's life as full of possibility and potential. As a result he developed mighty creative ways of getting around the house, brushing his teeth, feeding himself, and doing daily tasks. Surprisingly, he never gave up hope though he obviously looked noticeably different than others. It would have been easy to belief that he is odd, peculiar, out of place, and different and will ever have any chance at accomplishing what others can but this was not what Nick did. Instead he chose to persevere. He became an expert swimmer and surfer even eventually marrying a lady who also was without an arm. He now speaks at Christian motivational events to encourage others who feel like they have some type of impediments in their lives about being overcomers and thinking of possibilities.

Another great example to consider is Joni Erikson Tada. A girl who was a promising Olympian swimmer soon had that dream come to an end when she had an accident through which she became paralyzed. Initially she struggled with becoming angry and bitter at God for the life she though she should have. But in the long run as she embraced what she could not control she made peace with the idea of being the best as she was. Since that time thousands of people have been ministered to by seeing her speak with confidence from a wheelchair about God's goodness. Her faith has never been shattered. Though one dream seemed to end she is able to see how even life's surprises become way for God to use each of us in special ways for His glory.

Then there's the story of Dave Roever. This man went through severe situations on the battlefield which left him with facial deformities. His active duty combat experience was one that could have left severe emotional scars for life. Yet in spite of noticeable facial scars he refuses to succumb to Post Traumatic Stress reactions. He allows Jesus Christ to assist him in actively ministering to other active duty combat forces and army men and women in training. His speeches are not about the bitterness and regret he has towards his army days, anger towards the government, or unforgiveness for a life where he will never look a certain way. He declares and walks in an inner strength that no outside disfigurement can take away.

The beliefs of hopelessness, depression, defeat, and suicide in general will lead you or I to convince ourselves that these "success stories" can never be us. The issue, however, is not that people who succeed do not feel real hurt, pain, and have real life struggles but that they put them in perspective. Rather than the struggles defining them they see beyond the struggles. Even when they are so brokenhearted that they honestly can't see beyond the struggles they admit this to God and ask God for a larger sense of perspective not ruled by emotions of the moment alone.

There is a choice involved. Think of it this way. If you hold a pad of paper right up to your eyes all you see is the paper. It is magnified. You don't notice that there is a room behind the paper because that is hidden from view. But is only what is seen to our senses the whole truth? Of course not. When the paper is held at arm's length away from your eyes you see the paper. You have freedom to move forward on your healing journey when you do not deny the stress, struggles, and sometimes heart wrenching pain but still see a world beyond that. You also move on the path to freedom when you admit that you may not have answers or know the next step but you believe more than "this awful place is it. That's all there is to life."

I can hear some of you thinking that this is easy to say if a person had not gone through all you have. But the same is true. Maybe you were raped and incested so many times that it would have been natural to never trust a living soul. Perhaps you have struggled with bouts sickness that would leave someone hopeless. Maybe you have lost homes, jobs, and family leaving you feeling alone and destitute. It can be hard to see anything good at the time. It definitely feels miserable and far different than good or pleasant. It may feel like you even question what there is to live for anymore.

But what if you have not seen what God has beyond where you are at today? What if all of us can only see a portion with our eyes – that painful portion- but if we could see clearer we would see the other side. Though it may take some time it would come.

Jesus was an example of seeing beyond intense immediate pain in his own life. Betrayed by those who were supposed to be his best friends he was turned over to a ruthless, brutal death he did not deserve. His death was so brutal that his bones were able to be seen, his insides hanging out! Talk about a serious reason to say, "forget it! If I know I am going through this then I'm done. Let me do myself in!" Why face the pain? But there would not have been a resurrection day without the awful, brutal pain.

Did you ever consider this new life-giving belief? There is no possibility of a resurrection day- a day of hope and newness- without death of hopes and dreams, ending of some toxic once cherished relationships, life stresses, abuses and traumas, trials, and unimaginable hurts and pains. Something usually has to end or die or feel stagnant for there to be that new beginning. It takes a darkest hour experience to breed enough discontent to believe there has to be something else.

It is all about belief. If you focus on how life should have been then you will surely get stuck in the self-pity mindset but on the other hand if you focus on what life can be and will be in time by God's grace then you will eventually see some of the newness and life as God imagined it for you.

There is no possibility of a resurrection day- a day of hope and newness- without death of hopes and dreams, ending of some toxic once cherished relationships, life stresses, abuses and traumas, trials, and unimaginable hurts and pains. Something usually has to end or die or feel stagnant for there to be that new beginning. It takes a darkest hour experience to breed enough discontent to believe there has to be something else.

What I Confess

Not only are your beliefs and thoughts important but what you confess is critical. Think of your words as a seal on what you believe. It is one thing to think something but quite another to say it. When something is said it is declaring it is so. It is making a statement that a belief must therefore be true.

For example if you have received a negative diagnosis from the doctors about a terminal illness you have a choice about how you report this to your friends. You can report the doctor's findings in a neutral way. Alternatively, you can talk about how your life is over and your hopes are dashed. In this second example you are living as if you are already dead. A third option also exists. You can live life to the fullest and possibly surprise the doctors by living far beyond their predictions to where the diagnosis may even be in remission.

What if you have experienced loss after loss? It may be easy to expect another loss. In fact, expecting trauma, poor treatment and unhappiness in life may seem second nature to you. Maybe you never knew your parents. Maybe the foster parents you had were abusive. Maybe the people who were supposed to be friends betrayed you deeply. Maybe the few support systems who were consistently there for you all died too soon and left you alone. While these are certainly painful events you have some choices of reactions. You can choose to confess, "my life is over. I have no one." By this confession you are living as if you are dead with your deceased loved ones. However, there is another possible reaction. You can choose to enroll in a grief support group, find a hobby where you can make the possibly closest friendships ever or mentor others who have also needed motivation to go on.

There are options. The options often do not feel easy to implement. These alternatives may not be the first thing that comes to your mind in the moment. In the moment voices of self-pity, entitlement, and emotional destructiveness will try to speak that you have no options. You are sick. You must hurt. You must die.

What if you confess the spiritually sound truth, "No, I must live. I may not know how but day by day, moment by moment I must live?" I think of the Bible verses (Psalm 37:23-25) which say:

> The steps of a good man are ordered by the LORD: and he delights in his way. Though he fall, he shall not be utterly cast down: for the LORD upholds him with his hand. I have been young, and now am old; yet have I not seen the righteous forsaken, nor his seed begging bread.

One of the best lessons I learned as young Christian was about these steps. All too often ambitious people such as myself hate steps and want life to all fall in place rather quickly. But what if God wanted to do a "whole, complete and perfect work" (James 1:4) beyond the haphazard stuff you and I try to do? What if he loves you do much that He longs to take time to order the steps even if it means one month on step one and six months on step two or one year on step three so that by two years from now you look back as that renewed person marvelling at the amazing work none of us in our own self will could have done or created?

Process is painful and often there is no quick and easy way around it. Process feels like our enemy. If you are like me you may not see at the time anything good in process. Process means waiting. Process means not knowing.

Process means you and I have no control over anything but our own lives. Process means that though you may not know all the details as to how the troubles will end you have to keep persevering.

I laugh to think about the way James 1:1-5 describes the church greeting each other when they were in process:

> James, a servant of God and of the Lord Jesus Christ, to the twelve tribes which are scattered abroad, greeting. My brethren, count it all joy when ye fall into divers temptations; Knowing this, that the trying of your faith works patience. But let patience have her perfect work, that oue may be perfect and entire, wanting nothing. If any of you lack wisdom, let him ask of God, that giveth to all men liberally, and upbraids not; and it shall be given him.

A man named James talked about actually choosing to find something to appreciate during a process which requires patience. This is beyond ourselves. Our self-will without God's supernatural ability in and through us will keep us limited and frustrated. But I like the next part about being "perfected and lacking nothing." Perfecting never happens without process.

The hardest thing to be perfected in us according to the Bible is our speech. Proverbs 18:21 tells us that "death and life are in the power of the tongue: and they that love it shall eat the fruit thereof." This is a pretty powerful statement. It means that our words provide fuel to the fire so to speak. They either fuel the depression and the suicidal plan or attempt or they fuel the recovery. Sometimes learning to believe and speak differently is where it begins.

James 3:1-10 gives a description regarding the power and purpose of the tongue to destroy or build up:

My brethren, be not many masters, knowing that we shall receive the greater condemnation. For in many things we offend all. If any man offend not in word, the same is a perfect man, and able also to bridle the whole body. Behold, we put bits in the horses' mouths, that they may obey us; and we turn about their whole body. Behold also the ships, which though they be so great, and are driven of fierce winds, yet are they turned about with a very small helm. Even so the tongue is a little member, and boasts great things. Behold, how great a matter a little fire kindles! And the tongue is a fire, a world of iniquity: so is the tongue among our members, that it defiles the whole body, and sets on fire the course of nature; and it is set on fire of hell. For every kind of beasts, and of birds, and of serpents, and of things in the sea, is tamed, and hath been tamed of mankind: But the tongue can no man tame; it is an unruly evil, full of deadly poison. Therewith bless we God, even the Father; and therewith curse we men, which are made after the similitude of God. Out of the same mouth proceeds blessing and cursing. My brethren, these things ought not so to be.

Messages That Keep People Oppressed

Often there are thoughts and beliefs that seem to make sense to us on the surface but deep down keep us angry, stressed, resentful, upset, bitter, and stuck. These beliefs are so common to most people that at first glance they may actually seem rational and reasonable. However, as they are looked at more closely one can notice that there is a hook which keeps us in a place that takes us deeper into sadness darkness, anxiety, pain, and even utter despair. The key is seeing these automatic nice sounding phrases and thought patterns for what they really are- nothing more than lies and part truths.

The Bible in 1 John 4:1 tells us to "test the spirits, whether they are of God; because many false prophets have gone out into the world." This means that not all automatic feeling reactions (even when they are strong and persistent) are Biblical, Godly, and conducive to the abundant life God intended for us.

As we take a look at some of these common beliefs and part truths it is likely you will find yourself in some, if not many, of them. This does not mean you are doomed.

It means you are human and in need of an alternative, realistic, Godly perspective that will tell you the whole truth. It is never too late to be yielded and transformed when you discover pitfalls in your thinking.

Nice, good, helpful, kind, or ethical people deserve only good, happy, nice things to happen to them.

Many of you consider ourselves to be relatively kind, nice, ethical people. You believe that as such you should get some benefit over people out who may be more cold-hearted, malicious, or evil. Makes sense, doesn't it? Good people should get good things and bad people should get bad things. You and I are usually taught this from young childhood on. Be a "good girl or boy" and life will go well but if you are "bad" there will be a price to pay. The reality of life, however, is that it is not our "good" behaviors that get us what we think we should have in life. Biblically we are told that if we had a measuring stick about how "good" all of us are even by our own standards we would miserably fail. For example, Romans 3:22-25 states:

> Even the righteousness of God which is by faith of Jesus Christ unto all and upon all them that believe: for there is no difference: For all have sinned, and come short of the glory of God; Being justified freely by his grace through the redemption that is in Christ Jesus: Whom God hath set forth to be a propitiation through faith in his blood, to declare his righteousness for the remission of sins that are past, through the forbearance of God;

The key part that you and I need to focus on is that "all have sinned." None of us is "good enough" to achieve heaven on our own. Likewise, none of us if open to the message of the cross of Jesus Christ is "bad enough" to have God's compassion and forgiveness unavailable to him or her. That is what mercy and compassion are all about.

God chose you. You with all your flaws and imperfections. You with all your bad decisions and sins. You with all your detours, impulsive decisions, and u-turns. You who have messed up. He chose the flawed and messed up you whether at your worst or best to have an importunity to have equal access to all He has to give His children once you repent and choose to be changed and yielded to Him. The world may measure all of us in term of how superficially "good" or bad" you are but God judges what is inside your heart. 1 Samuel 16:7 states it this way:

But the LORD said unto Samuel, Look not on his countenance, or on the height of his stature; because I have refused him: for the LORD sees not as man sees; for man looks on the outward appearance, but the LORD looks on the heart.

Only God accurately judges the rationales behind what you label "good" behavior. By reviewing the aforementioned example, for instance, you can observe that there are people you might rule out as "too bad" who God chooses to use in spite of themselves. There are also people you and I can think are good, and kind, favored and liked outwardly which may not be God's preference. This is because He knows the heart.

You and I think we know someone's heart well if we have had several conversations with that person. We think we know a person by observing that person's behaviors for some time. However, only God accurately sees those inner motives with a clarity that we do not have.

This is a refreshing and sobering encouragement to us today. Since God knows your heart and motivations he also knows if you were hurt unjustly. He will fight for you. He will favor your heart if it is inclined toward His ways in spite of what other people believe about you. God's justice and mercy are perfect. He knows the real you that you may not show others. He knows the you behind the smiles that hurt deep inside. He knows the you who acts "strong" but feels anything but strong. He knows the you who has persevered with strength beyond yourself. He knows the sacrifices you have made. He knows those secret moments not even your best friend is aware of. Not only does He know those instances but He cherishes the ability to walk through every one of them with you.

In spite of knowing the whole complete story about the inner you He has chosen to put your "goodness" or "badness" on His cross. Instead, He has replaced it with His righteousness meaning that if you will allow Him to speak the truth about who you are and what direction is needed in your life, He will renew you. He will forget the past sins and "bad" and even "cast them in the sea of forgetfulness." (Micah 7:19) He will also overlook the good you claim to be and have. He will judge you based on how you respond sincerely to His replacing your inadequacy with His adequacy, your sin with His purity, and your worst and best with His perfection and holiness.

This belief about being "good" or "bad" is also dangerous because it puts you in a very subjective judgment. How would any of us know if we have been "good" or "bad" enough? According to whom? By what standards?

God chose you. You with all your flaws and imperfections. You with all your bad decisions and sins. You with all your detours, impulsive decisions, and u-turns. You who have messed up. He chose the flawed and messed up you whether at your worst or best to have an importunity to have equal access to all He has to give His children

Thank God that He is the God of second chances. Thank God that He waits on us to respond to His completed, finished, perfect work of mercy when our work has many shortcomings. I bet that thief on the cross who repented in his last, dying moments was thankful that it was not because of his natural earthly "goodness" that Jesus decided the thief's fate. Rather, Jesus seeing the sincerity of heart in the once criminal man stated, "this very day you will be with me in paradise." (Luke 23:43) I bet Paul who was once known as Saul, the mass murderer of Christians, was forever grateful that someone saw potential in his to be something other than an angry, rage-filled, hateful murderer. Even when other religious folk still saw him as "non-good" based on his past murders God used him after he yielded to God as a great traveling evangelist and church planter, a father of the faith to many. Thank God that Peter, a disciple who walked closely with Jesus yet denied even knowing Him when times got hard was not judge solely on this "not good" betrayal. Rather, Jesus used this broken and humbled man who afterward recognized that he could be just as prone to sin as someone else without the Lord's guidance in the moment to be the first pastor of the New Testament church. A young lady names Mary who was just developing life skills in her teens and had not matured physically and in terms of life experience was chosen to be the vessel to carry the body of baby Jesus. A poor widow who had nothing but gave a simple coin, her all, was used as model to the religious folk who considered their superficial "good" as greater. Jesus disagreed and said that the widow gave from her nothingness with sincerity.

Only God can develop within you a truly good heart. If you read the Beatitudes in Matthew 5:1-12 you hear over and over "blessed are those who...." We don't hear about the outwardly good but we hear about people who are favored of God because they are yielded and because of hearts cultivated by God:

> And seeing the multitudes, he went up into a mountain: and when he was set, his disciples came unto him: And he opened his mouth, and taught them, saying, Blessed are the poor in spirit: for theirs is the kingdom of heaven. Blessed are they that mourn: for they shall be comforted. Blessed are the meek: for they shall inherit the earth. Blessed are they which do hunger and thirst after righteousness: for they shall be filled. Blessed are the merciful: for they shall obtain mercy. Blessed are the pure in heart: for they shall see God. Blessed are the peacemakers: for they shall be called the children of God. Blessed are they which are persecuted for righteousness' sake: for theirs is the kingdom of heaven. Blessed are ye, when men shall revile you, and persecute you, and shall say all manner of evil against you falsely, for my sake. Rejoice, and be exceeding glad: for great is your reward in heaven.

There is no reason that your heart cannot be one He shapes and molds today to be loving, kind, patient, gracious, self-controlled, peaceable, holy, etc .

If we pray right now with sincerity as David did, "Lord, create within me a clean and new heart and renew a right spirt within me" God will respond (see Psalm 51:10). He will create genuine goodness that is not a matter of will power and outward actions but is a state of humble, innocent, sincere making of one amazing and tremendous beautiful heart in you.

I have had more than my share of bad, stressful stuff. I can't handle any more.

Life can be so unpredictable. You and I are never promised a certain quota of stressful things versus peaceful times. We tend to become lax when the plateaus come. We forget that the strength and source which enabled us to go a step further had nothing to do with us ourselves but everything to do with our mighty God. We return to thinking silly, ridiculous stuff like that we could ever "handle" anything anyway. What we thought was handling things was really life gong along okay in spite of us.

The mistake we tend to make is that we think that it is because of us that life can be made to be calm and easy. But it is really never because of us controlling, fixing, and being acceptable people that things are able to be handled. It is more truthful to say that, in spite of our best and worst, life goes along anyway.

There is a Bible verse that personally has been pretty annoying for me but rings true where the stressors don't seem to die down though you faithfully keep persevering. Scripture says, "for he makes his sun to rise on the evil and on the good, and sends rain on the just and on the unjust." (Matthew 5:45) This means that everyone gets some enjoyment and some okay peaceful times in life, everyone gets some times of fun, rejoicing, and where things seem to go well for a while. Everyone gets some plateaus where the stresses seem to die down for a while. Finally, everyone gets the crud of life too. No one is immune to junk happening. There are unexpected surprises for all of us.

Managing life is less about being a manager and more about being a student who is teachable as a disciple of the Lord. As such, stressors do not have to be the mark of doom. Have you ever noticed that some of the most resilient, hope filled and optimistic people have survived pain, traumas and unexpected circumstances? It is all about choice and perspective. In fact, some people even submit to the process to where they do not just endure trials but they grow and thrive. They learn new skills, they adapt to situations. They find resources they may not have known of before. They try new ways of handling things. They admit that it was never because of self that they made it through but in spite of them and that in spite of them they will make it through again.

When troubles come there's a choice. Person #1 may think, "here comes more pain. I can't get beyond this. This is the last straw." He or she may give up. On the other hand, person #2 may think, "interesting. Another opportunity for a miracle. Another crazy thing that is beyond me that my God will have to figure out." That second person will be sitting waiting with eager anticipation because he or she knows that behind the surprises of life there are hidden doors of opportunity.

I've waited far too long for things to turn around (e.g. job, finances, health, relationships). I should not have any dry times, waiting, or wilderness experiences where the things I want and need are not actively unfolding before my eyes.

You and I are a people who hate to wait. And you have probably been told that you shouldn't have to wait. You may only end up more frustrated in life when you are bombarded by T.V, commercials and advertisements around you that tell you that if you deserve something then you should get it. Not only should you get it, but you should also get it immediately. Any delay or waiting period is awful. As a result, like stubborn young children fighting for a favorite toy you and I kick and scream inside for things we believe we should never do without.

Have you ever noticed that some of the most resilient, hope filled and optimistic people have survived pain, traumas and unexpected circumstances? It is all about choice and perspective. In fact, some people even submit to the process to where they do not just endure trials but they grow and thrive. They learn new skills, they adapt to situations. They find resources they may not have known of before. They try new ways of handling things. They admit that it was never because of self that they made it through but in spite of them and that in spite of them they will make it through again.

Could there possibly be any benefit to waiting? Could there remotely be any good thing behind the idea of delayed gratification?

The Bible talks about "times and seasons" a lot. It uses phrases like "at the appropriate time", "in due time", "and at the appointed time." I have come to realize that no matter how uncomfortable the waiting and how much I do not understand how the delay is beneficial to me it is better that I wait for the full, complete, and appropriate timing of the things God wants for me to be manifest. Scripture in James 1:4 refers to God doing a whole, complete, and perfect work through the process of my life. When I am inpatient, crabby, and insisting on my way I am essentially saying, "I know better than anyone else. Who cares about God's perfect and complete work. I'll take the quick and sloppy work just so I can be what I want how I want in the timing I want."

And sometimes because we are stubborn we have to learn the hard way God allows us to. He had to do this, for example, with the Israelites. A journey of 11 days ended up taking thee 40 years because they had their own ideas about several issues along the way. They wanted things a certain way in a certain timing. Even when God provided a best way they refused essentially and did not yield because it was not the way they desired.

So let's look at some of the Scriptures regarding waiting. Lamentations 3:25 says, "The Lord is good unto them that wait for him, to the soul that seeks him." We think the good is what does not require anything from us. Have you ever noticed that when you have to wait for something you tend to really appreciate it more when it happens? Imagine if you did not have to save up money for things over the curse of months or years. You may not appreciate that item you wish to buy and the value of hard work along the way. Imagine if you got everything you wanted how you wanted. You may end up in some awful relationships with people you were never meant to have. You may end up in some towns and cities you were never meant to go to. You may end up with some attitudes that produce more confusion and unhappiness.

How do I know this? Because throughout time people have essentially been the same. They would often rather get in a mess and have what they desire then have to try and patch it up later. But later comes with much grief. People in Bible days were just as stubborn, self-willed, and impatient as they are today. The nature of people essentially has not changed.

Thankfully the nature of God also has not changed. That's why waiting and yelling in the frustration is never worth it. Psalm 37:7-9 encourages us to:

> Rest in the LORD, and wait patiently for him: fret not thyself because of him who prospers in his way, because of the man who brings wicked devices to pass. Cease from anger, and forsake wrath: fret not thyself in any ways to do evil. For evildoers shall be cut off: but those that wait upon the LORD, they shall inherit the earth.

Isaiah 40:31 is also a frequently quoted Scripture which reminds us of the value amidst the discomfort in waiting. It declares that "they that wait upon the LORD shall renew their strength; they shall mount up with wings as eagles; they shall run, and not be weary; and they shall walk, and not faint."

There was something in my own life God showed me one day which has always stuck with me. It was during a time where I was arguing with God about how long I had waited on some things and how I should have them now. I talked with God about how the pain of delay was too much to bear. I even tried to make a case before God that I had really waited on him. God's reaction to me in prayer was very enlightening. He caused me to see that all the time I thought I was waiting on Him I really was praying to Him but still waiting on people and circumstances to do the right, Godly things. He illuminated to me something, "If you are really waiting on me, why are you so frustrated with people, places, and things around you? Why are you angry and disappointed when things do not line up and they do not obey Me? Are you waiting on me or are you waiting on people to do something, circumstances to be a certain way?"

After this realization I had to admit that God knows me far better than I would like to admit. Renewed strength in the waiting will never come from our negotiations and arguments. You and I can never prove to God why our timing is better than His. The only time we will truly be refreshed, renewed, and strengthened is in waiting on Him.

The other realization you and I often forget is that there is less than perfect joy and fulfillment when we get things in our own way and time. We may be happy from getting what we want but even in that happiness there is no real contentment and fulfillment.

Have you ever witnessed this? It feels awful when eventually God backs away because we argue so much about something and want our way. He allows us to possibly get that thing, relationship, or goal but in a less than ideal way. So while we are complaining about the stress we are having He is crying out "but remember you wanted it this way! You wanted this person, this job, this thing, this way."

What's the alternative to selfish thinking? The alternative which brings immediate inconvenience but long term contentment and fulfillment is "leaning on the Lord with all your understanding." Proverbs 3:5-6 says, "Trust in the Lord with all thine heart; and lean not unto thine own understanding. In all thy ways acknowledge him, and he shall direct thy paths." Psalm 31:15 also says, "My times are in thy hand: deliver me from the hand of mine enemies, and from them that persecute me. You, O Lord; I said, You are my God. My times are in Your hands."

This is the same cry of Jesus at Gesthemane- facing the most impending, cruel death. He cries out "Father, not my will but yours be done." Hear him crying out with you in your waiting, "if you can take this painful cup from _____." He is with you as you cry out about the painful, stressful waiting. He also wants to be with you as He who first went to Gesthemane strengthens you to say "not my will but yours be done."

Life is unfair and unjust. Other people always get ahead of me but my life is always bad.

We really have a double standard, don't we? We are quick to want to put a nail in the coffin of the person who did something wrong to us because they need justice. However, when it comes to our own guilt in offenses we are quick to justify why we deserve mercy and forgiveness. We realize the hurt and pain offenses are to us when we believe they are caused by other people but we often do not take the time to reflect on how our own behaviors may likewise have caused offenses to others.

It feels awful when eventually God backs away because we argue so much about something and want our way. He allows us to possibly get that thing, relationship, or goal but in a less than ideal way. So while we are complaining about the stress we are having He is crying out "but remember you wanted it this way! You wanted this person, this job, this thing, this way."

We tend to assume that others know exactly what they have done to us and yet continue doing it anyway purposefully. However, we wish to be given the benefit of the doubt about our own behavior. Surely we didn't really mean to maliciously hurt someone.

I think about what Jesus said on the cross. He stated, "Father, forgive them for they know not what they have done." (Luke 23:32) When I thought about all the events leading to the crucifixion I thought, "God surely they do know what they have done. They knew they were hurting you. They know they were beating and wounding you. They knew but they don't care." However, after much prayer and Bible research I have come to realize that there is much more beyond this statement. Jesus is saying, "they may know on the surface what they are doing but they don't really know the implications of it." Many of those who handed him to be crucified over Barabus did not understand that this was the Messiah right before their eyes. Many of the religious leaders who bought Jesus from Judas did not realize that all their hours of studying over the scrolls could not recognize this one who was living and walking among them. Even the disciples who walked moment by moment with Jesus did not always know who Jesus fully was. In fact Jesus asked, "who do you say I am?" (Mark 8:29)

Likewise, often times you or I think we are only reacting to an immediate issue in our own limited reaction. We do not frequently see the deep spiritual implications of such actions. To us we are justly yelling at, punishing, and giving the other what he or she deserves. All the while we are turning people over to what seem to be logical consequences for us but do not tell the whole story. Might there have been a reason that one yelled at you? Might someone have been having stress in their life which made them more snappy than usual? Might they have been in an unusual situation of which you do not have all the details? Might they "have moments" just like we "have our moments?"

What if, as an alternative we considered the behavior suggested in the Lord's prayer. "Forgive us our trespasses as we forgive them." Note the key phrase "as we forgive them." (Matthew 6:9-13) Elsewhere in Scripture we are reminded that when someone is forgiven much he or she tends to be more sensitive to the plight of others. (Luke 7:47) Maybe it would be a god idea for us to reflect on what we have been forgiven of in God's book. As you reflect on those things I encourage you to not think in terms of a hierarchy as if your offenses are "only little sins" compared to others "big" offenses.

What might it be like if we really allowed for the justice and the mercy to Jesus Christ who judges and has compassion perfectly and with full knowledge, understanding, and wisdom? Sure, it might feel a little helpless to us because we all have our own judgments. On the other hand, aren't situations better left in Jesus' hand which holds the nail scarred victory of resurrection than our hands which tend to keep offenses going?

I must be loved by all those who matter to me or I cannot be content with myself.

Biblically God often uses people in our lives as a source of encouragement to reach out to us. In fact, He speaks quite a bit about being edifying and speaking truth to one another. Often times it is those people who we are most in direct relationships with who become to us as "God in the flesh." But the problem is that people all have their own fallacies. They don't love us when they are supposed to. They don't encourage and edify when they should.

They don't always give Godly counsel. They don't listen at times when they just need to be supportive. They reject God's direct commands in Scripture pertaining to how they should treat us. They don't speak the truth in love at times either. In other words, they are human just like us.

The fact is anyone and everyone who is closest to you in your life will let you down. One way or another people will not reflect God as they should. One way or another you will be left alone to encourage yourself in the Lord. That is probably the toughest thing to do. The worst part about it is that usually it happens at the times when you feel you need that human connection most. When you are at your weakest it can be particularly challenging to come up with anything to keep yourself going.

People may not be purposely letting you down. People may simply not be able to read your mind and know your needs. People may not have the resources to meet your needs in the way you expect. People may define love, caring, and kindness in differing terms than you.

This is why there is a responsibility we each must take for our own happiness. Only you know exactly what you want or need. It is your responsibility for identifying and communicating those needs. You also have responsibility for limiting your contacts with people who are not life giving supports towards those needs. In addition, you may need to seek out new support systems. Perhaps the most important realization though is that your outlook is more important than what people say or do. If things are not working, you can be willing to do something different or new. You can, by the grace of God and with your personal goals in mind, do less of what is not working and develop a higher frequency of what works.

Besides taking some responsibility for our own happiness you and I can also benefit from understanding the background of the word "contentment" Scripturally. The Bible talks about a life of relying on what you know to be spiritually true by faith. This means starting with the fact that God is well able to take all your issues and concerns on and deal with them perfectly. His Word and promises cannot return void. Isaiah 55:15 emphatically tells us, "So shall my word be that goes forth out of my mouth: it shall not return unto me void, but it shall accomplish that which I please, and it shall prosper in the thing whereto I sent it." He knows better than ourselves and people around us what we need as well as how to meet those needs.

You can still rely on God as your peace even when everything and everyone around us is stirring and disrupting things. Philippians chapter 4 promises Christ's peace as we think upon what is true, honest, just, pure, lovely, and of good report:

> Rejoice in the Lord always: and again I say, Rejoice. Let your moderation be known unto all men. The Lord is at hand. Be careful for nothing; but in everything by prayer and supplication with thanksgiving let your requests be made known unto God. And the peace of God, which passes all understanding, shall keep your hearts and minds through Christ Jesus. Finally, brethren, whatsoever things are true, whatsoever things are honest, whatsoever things are just, whatsoever things are pure, whatsoever things are lovely, whatsoever things are of good report; if there be any virtue, and if there be any praise, think on these things. Those things, which ye have both learned, and received, and heard, and seen in me, do: and the God of peace shall be with you.

Thinking on what other people have or have not been to us will not bring peace. It will only bring utter disappointment. It will only make us feel like never trusting another soul. It will only make us want to give up on people out there.

It is possible then through encouraging yourself in the Lord for you to have hope in the midst of all things. Then, if others around additionally add encouragement, love, longsuffering, kindness and goodness, it will be a bonus. But if not, you will have God do so.

David was a man who suffered with much depression, a man of many tears and much grief. The bouts of despair and being downcast were many. He was inclined himself to think about the enemies of God and the wicked people around and injustices. It got to him. But his response is what we can notice and use as our help. He sang and worshipped the Lord nonetheless. He fixed his eyes not on what was around him but rather on "the Author and Finisher of his faith" (Hebrews 12:2). In Psalms you hear a transition from the first half of depression, tears drenching his pillow, hopelessness, helplessness, anger, rage, and depression to glimmers of hope as he reflects on the God who is there "in spite of."

Let me encourage you in your mess to likewise encourage yourself by focusing on the God who is all by himself there for you completely and perfectly in spite of what is around you. Even if you happen to have the most amazing support system in the world they can never come close to God. He is ever present and ever available. He wants for us to ask and knock and seek. Matthew 7:7-11 beckons us to do this:

Ask, and it shall be given you; seek, and ye shall find; knock, and it shall be opened unto you: For every one that asks receives; and he that seeks finds; and to him that knocks it shall be opened. Or what man is there of you, whom if his son ask bread, will he give him a stone? Or if he ask a fish, will he give him a serpent? If ye then, being evil, know how to give good gifts unto your children, how much more shall your Father which is in heaven give good things to them that ask him?

God guarantees He will respond when we call on Him. His answers may be an array of different responses but they will ultimately even when uncomfortable be "good gifts."

When you feel like you have no support systems round about you remember that you still have the best support person ever. Hear today in your heart as when Jesus spoke it to his disciples years ago a personal and direct message to you: "I will not leave you comfortless: I will come to you." (John 14:18) Rather than waiting for those around you to be what they were supposed to be count on the One who is who He says He is. God is not like people who have let you down. Numbers 23:19 assures us that "God is not a man that he should lie; neither the son of man, that he should repent: hath he said, and shall he not do it? or hath he spoken, and shall he not make it good?" When your spouse is not Christ to you, when your family deserts you, when friends are few, when the church is not the New Testament church for you, and when it is hard to believe in anyone or anything, God still is there enabling you even now to believe the truth about yourself and your situations.

This pain and discomfort is too much.

One of the toughest issues for all of us is distinguishing between how things feel and how they are supernaturally. When layers of life upon layers pile up the discomfort and be utterly overwhelming. It can be so far beyond us. If we rely on our natural strength and resources we would collapse.

Do you recall the Scriptures about "casting your care on Jesus?" 1 Peter 5:7 directs us to "humble yourselves therefore under the mighty hand of God, that he may exalt you in due time:." Psalm 55:22 also instructs us to "cast thy burden upon the LORD, and he shall sustain thee: he shall never suffer the righteous to be moved." Did you catch that key word "never?" This means then that if you and I are moved it is our feelings and emotions, our concentrating around us, our distractibility which is moving us. We have a choice here then about whether we allow ourselves to be moved or not. You may not have had that choice about horrible circumstances you have faced but you have a choice about the degree to which those circumstances move you.

Normally you and I get moved when we start thinking that the awful circumstance is the last determining chapter of our life. It's all gloom and doom. We are stuck. We have no control. But we can instead admit that this chapter of the story of our lives may be unexpected, painful or uncertain. That does not have to mean that a next chapter is not meanwhile being written which is better, more hopeful, and offers a renewed sense of perspective on life.

If you and I are supposed to be relieved we just read that we must become better at casting. *Casting* means to throw with force. Let's practice this. Imagine writing on pieces of paper one by one each stress and burden and issue facing you. Write down about your cancer, your pain, your financial problems, your relationship issues, your emotional pain, everything. Then one by one crumple those papers up as tight as you can. Talk to God as you do it. Cry if you need to. Then go alone with God and start casting each of these on Him.

Of course crumpling papers in and of by itself will offer only some relief. But the idea is that as you are doing this representative action you are throwing with force the weights off you. You are deciding to stop holding the burden of fixing and figuring out what you cannot control. For added effect I have even had some people use actual little stones or rocks for this exercise. On each stone a word is painted representing a different stress or issue. Then the stones are put in a container which is presented symbolically to God. Some people prefer this rocks idea because they can actually physically feel the weight each one ads to where more rocks become a struggle to carry.

I have seen several people experience deliverance and healing in this exercise just feeling the weight leave them physically and dumping it on Christ. I have seen people in my office cry tears of happiness and freedom, dance, shout for joy, praise the Lord and report for weeks and months ongoing freedom as they were able to visually see a representation of what spiritually has happened with God carrying their trash away. What is weighting you down now? What is making you feel like you are under more than you can handle? Come out now from under the weight of the world!!!

Remember there is one named Jesus Christ who took that weight already and who is ready for all your stuff to be thrown on Him. Tell Him as you pray that you can't take it anymore. Grieve the losses. Ask the difficult questions. Speak the needs.

Then after throwing with force on Him all those cares take time to listen. Pause. Let Him respond to it all. Allow yourself to rest in the knowledge that He just got your crud piled on Him. Don't be surprised if He gives you instructions. He may tell you Scriptural instructions regarding what Biblical principles you need to continue walking in to be healed and whole while you let Him do His job behind the scenes. Resist the urge to pick the stuff you cast on Him back up. That is like saying, "I don't trust you. I think I can handle it better, God. I have not done the best this far but I would rather hold it than believe what you say."

Hear today in your heart as when Jesus spoke it to his disciples years ago a personal and direct message to you: "I will not leave you comfortless: I will come to you." (John 14:18) Rather than waiting for those around you to be what they were supposed to be count on the One who is who He says He is. God is not like people who have let you down. Numbers 23:19 assures us that "God is not a man that he should lie; neither the son of man, that he should repent: hath he said, and shall he not do it? or hath he spoken, and shall he not make it good?" When your spouse is not Christ to you, when your family deserts you, when friends are few, when the church is not the New Testament church for you, and when it is hard to believe in anyone or anything, God still is there enabling you even now to believe the truth about yourself and your situations.

Good People Hurt Too

The Bible is full of people just like me and you with depression, moodswings, impatience, physical ailments, distrust, temptations, strongholds, and all sorts of promises. That is what makes it even more beautiful. God always chooses what the Bible calls foolish vessels to do His work through. This is so that all the glory only goes to Him. He chooses people who do not have hope on their own. He chooses people who have no strength left. He chooses people who cry all night and are emotionally unstable. He chooses people with fleshly temptations and lusts. He chooses people who think they know better than God about life choices. He chooses people whose own human natures are far, far different from God's infinite, perfect ways. While God does not endorse or approve of sinful behaviors or attitudes and wants to deliver people from them He chooses people who would be naturally bent on their own humanity that His light, His grace, Himself is then able to shine through.

One such example is David. Though called "a man after God's heart" (Acts 13:22) David was a person who cried a lot, complained a lot, and was tempted about women a lot. Sounds like a rather imperfect person to me. One reason David cried out about frequently to God was the fact that he felt like he was being oppressed by the wicked, godless fools who seemed to get ahead in life. He also cried out about "being under affliction" in Psalms 102 and other psalms. For example, we see the symptoms of depression when he says "his bones ache." He is fatigued and in physical pain as the chronic fatigue is getting to him. He says "my heart is struck down." This is hopelessness and discouragement. Even spiritual people can struggle with it because of the weight of issues and people around them. He suffers from a reduced appetite and lack of eating food. He specifically states, "I forget to eat my bread because of my loud groaning." Like a person depressed and anxious who is preoccupied with the pain and stresses of life he says he "lies awake all night." He also feels very alone.

If you ever doubt that these Bible people felt what you go through I suggest you actually read some of the words they said. Let's consider David's grumblings in Psalm 102: 1-20 as an example:

> Hear my prayer, O LORD, and let my cry come unto thee. Hide not thy face from me in the day when I am in trouble; incline thine ear unto me: in the day when I call answer me speedily. For my days are consumed like smoke, and my bones are burned as an hearth. My heart is smitten, and withered like grass; so that I forget to eat my bread. By reason of the voice of my groaning my bones cleave to my skin. I am like a pelican of the wilderness: I am like an owl of the desert. I watch, and am as a sparrow alone upon the house top. Mine enemies reproach me all the day; and they that are mad against me are sworn against me.

For I have eaten ashes like bread, and mingled my drink with weeping. Because of thine indignation and thy wrath: for thou hast lifted me up, and cast me down. My days are like a shadow and I am withered like grass. But thou, O Lord, shall endure forever; and thy remembrance unto all generations. Thou shalt arise, and have mercy upon Zion: for the time to favor her, yea, the set time, is come. For thy servants take pleasure in her stones, and favor the dust thereof. So the heathen shall fear the name of the Lord, and all the kings of the earth thy glory. When the Lord shall build up Zion, he shall appear in his glory. He will regard the prayer of the destitute, and not despise their prayer. This shall be written for the generation to come: and the people which shall be created shall praise the Lord. For he hath looked down from the height of his sanctuary; from heaven did the Lord behold the earth; To hear the groaning of the prisoner; to loose those that are appointed to death.

I wonder if any of this feels like where you may have been in your darkest hour. Have you ever felt smitten, withered, not wanted to eat or sleep, worried, destitute? Has your heart ever groaned inside from pain? Have you ever been so discouraged that you thought you were appointed to death instead of considering a better life ahead?

Hannah was another such Godly woman who really suffered with feeling abandoned and depressed. The Bible says she was "deeply distressed." It does not say she was just a little sad or barely disappointed. She was "deeply distressed." She had a longing that burned in her heart which was Godly but was not coming to pass. This longing was for Godly offspring which she could dedicate to God and raise in His service. At her first she was so disheartened about the cry of her heart ever manifesting that she "wept bitterly." She went to the priest and others who also did not relate or understand. They did not know how even though she trusted God with her prayer and hope she was genuinely hurting because nothing was happening. If you continue to read the story though eventually God manifests a turnaround for her and Samuel is born, a Godly young man raised and trained for the Lord's service. After seeing her husband's other wife at the time who was ungodly bearing child after child and being barren herself she wondered what was going on. While she knew of God's faithfulness deep in her heart the delay was nonetheless painful.

Let's read her example in 1 Samuel 1:9-11 so you can see how you are certainly not alone in hoping and wishing for some good desires for your life that may be taking more time than you expected:

Hannah, why weepest thou? and why eatest thou not? and why is thy heart grieved? ... So Hannah rose up after they had eaten in Shiloh, and after they had drunk. Now Eli the priest sat upon a seat by a post of the temple of the Lord. Now Hannah, she spoke in her heart; only her lips moved, but her voice was not heard: therefore Eli thought she had been drunken. And Hannah answered and said, No, my lord, I am a woman of a sorrowful spirit: I have drunk neither wine nor strong drink, but have poured out my soul before the Lord.

This is why it is so critical that we never put down people when they are waiting and clinging to God. We never know how long they have asked, waited, and trusted. We never know how many tears they have cried in secret. We never know how many nights they have drenched their pillow as David or how long they have waited for good promises they longed for as Hannah.

Another person who was God fearing but became depressed to the point of being even suicidal was Elijah. He specifically stated, "It is enough Lord. Now take my life." There is no other way to say that he was not at his wits end. He was so despondent even that he laid under a broom tree and slept. Have you ever come to the place all you at to do is stay in bed all day and night or hide away from everyone because of the pain you are going through? You are not alone.

But watch what happens next. It says in Scripture, "and behold, an angel touched him and said to him, 'Arise and eat.'" (1 Kings 19:5) Elijah was wearing away just lying under a tree and wishing to be dead. Maye you wear away in tears and depression under your bed covers. But even now God is telling you, "stop staying stuck." There are two critical pieces here. The first is "arise." We have to move physically and more importantly spiritually from the place of contemplating and wallowing in our very real pain to the place of receiving instruction to take a next step.

It is important to understand the meaning of the broom tree. The broom tree was used to escape the hot sun in the desert. The roots of this tree were also used for food and to prevent dehydration. In case you didn't know that when Elijah went there he was going there to run away from Jezebel. There may be people in your life as in mine who have been very abusive to where you just wanted to run away and be anywhere but around them.

However, when we understand the power and authority of the believer we will no longer look for a tree to sit under. We will come out from under the place of terror and fear and into the open under the hand of God's presence where there is comfort in His truth.

The second thing that happens is that Elijah is told to eat. So he has to get out from under his real self-pity and pain and move away from the false shelter of the pain of what he is going through. Then he has to do something he does not feel like doing-eat. If you have ever been depressed you know that it may take everything you've got to eat sleep, bathe, change your clothes, talk to people, go outside, or do the day to day. Yet that's exactly what the angel commanded Elijah to do. Sometimes we have to do what we do not feel like doing at all and God will honor it. Sometimes we have to do that before the people around us change or even if they don't change. Sometimes we have to do that when the problem situations are still there.

Another example we see in Scripture of the natural human response to pain is in our brother Paul. He stated in 2 Corinthians 1:8-10:

> For we would not, brethren, have you ignorant of our trouble which came to us in Asia, that we were pressed out of measure, above strength, insomuch that we despaired even of life: But we had the sentence of death in ourselves, that we should not trust in ourselves, but in God which raises the dead: Who delivered us from so great a death, and doth deliver: in whom we trust that he will yet deliver us.

In himself Paul and those he was with felt despair as stated here. But we again must distinguish between the real feeling which deserves to be empathized with and administered to and the actions God requires. Paul, after stating how he despaired of life itself, to go on to say that God who is the source of hope will deliver him and them again.

Of course we cannot forget Jesus' plight in the garden of Gesthemane. He was so stressed out that He had an extreme physical condition where he sweated blood. Now that is stress!!!!

> And he was withdrawn from them about a stone's cast, and kneeled down, and prayed, saying, Father, if thou be willing, remove this cup from me: nevertheless not my will, but thine, be done. And there appeared an angel unto him from heaven, strengthening him. And being in an agony he prayed more earnestly: and his sweat was as it were great drops of blood falling down to the ground.

Jesus' soul was overwhelmed. This is the Savior of the world, the sinless, spotless one saying this. In His soul based on the weight of the pains of life He is overwhelmed. He asks the Father to take the cup from Him. It is so pained emotionally that an angel has to come to strengthen Him. There had to be a transition even for Jesus from the choice to stay in the despair of the soul's darkest hour to the light which can only be found in the spirit man.

When we are under so much pain we see several key words frequently used in the Bible as well. The word *hamam* talks of the commotion and disturbance which brings trouble in one's life. It talks about being crushed and destroyed by the weight of life. Additionally, it carries with it the idea of an uproar or a loud agitation or noise which rings out. *Mhuwmah* is another Bible word referring to a similar concept of being in confusion and uproar with destruction, trouble, tumult, vexation, and discomfort all around. With this may also come what the Bible calls *timmahown* or bewilderment. For some people the pain may be so much that it may give way to *shigga/shiggari* or *halal* which mean insanity. For example, king Nebuchadnezzar was stricken by God with insanity (Daniel 4:31-33). Saul, however, became more psychotic and paranoid because of his jealousy, rage and anger toward David and his rebellion to God.

If unyielded to God in the midst of our dark times there's no saying what you or I may resort to. David, when he did not yield fully to God, resorted to lust and taking others' wives. King Saul of the Old Testament resorted to violent thoughts of murder like pinning David to the wall." (e.g. 1 Samuel 18:10-12) When Nebuchadnezzar did not yield to God and remained prideful he was stricken with dementia and loss of reason by God. He began eating grass like cattle, his body was drenched with the dew of heaven until his hair had grown like eagles' feathers and his nails like bird's claws.

But there is always good news in spite of the dark times. Let's take a look though at what happens when the prideful Nebuchadnezzar stop his pride and submits with humility to the Lord. Then he "raised his eyes to heaven and his reason returned and he blessed the Most High and praised and honored Hum who lives forever, for His dominion is an everlasting dominion and His kingdom lasts from generation to generation." (Daniel 4:31-34)

Even murderous Saul in the New Testament after an encounter with the Lord on the road to Damascus had to make a choice. When he realized the depths of his hatred and persecution toward the Lord's followers he made a drastic change. Acts 9:9-22 recounts this transition of when Saul allowed God to take him from dark times of an angry murderer to a new life:

And Saul, yet breathing out threatenings and slaughter against the disciples of the Lord, went unto the high priest, and desired of him letters to Damascus to the synagogues, that if he found any of this way, whether they were men or women, he might bring them bound unto Jerusalem. And as he journeyed, he came near Damascus: and suddenly there shined round about him a light from heaven: And he fell to the earth, and heard a voice saying unto him, Saul, Saul, why perse-cutest thou me? And he said, Who art thou, Lord? And the Lord said, I am Jesus whom thou perse-cutes: it is hard for thee to kick against the pricks. And he trembling and astonished said, Lord, what wilt thou have me to do? And the Lord said unto him, Arise, and go into the city, and it shall be told thee what thou must do. Then was Saul certain days with the disciples which were at Damascus. And straightway he preached Christ in the synagogues, that he is the Son of God. But all that heard him were amazed, and said; Is not this he that destroyed them which called on this name in Jerusalem, and came hither for that intent, that he might bring them bound unto the chief priests? But Saul increased the more in strength, and confounded the Jews which dwelt at Damascus, proving that this is very Christ.

The key to making the transition from the darkest hour to a new abundant life is what we allow to persist in our souls. There are things that should be warning signs to us that something is awry and needs to be submitted to the Lord. People who are prideful and think they need no one or that no one even giving Biblical advice can tell them anything should watch out. This includes people who are a "one man show" and want all attention and adoration but never allow Biblical rebuke or oversight of them. People who persist willingly in sin are also on dangerous ground. People who when the error if their ways Biblically is shown to them still refuse to repent are on dangerous ground. People who wallow in their depression, anxiety, pains, and stresses of life even when they are very real and substantiated are also on dangerous territory. Finally, people who are rebellious and refuse to revere the Holy, Almighty God through Jesus Christ are bound for long term trouble.

There is no denying when you feel it is a dark hour. Your Christian spouse and family, your church family, and anyone who calls themselves a Biblical follower of Christ should walk alongside you in your pain. We are commanded to do that after all. We are commanded to weep with those who are weeping and rejoice with those who are rejoicing. Now there is a line between empathy and understanding and condoning self-pity. Our job as believers is to hear the real pain someone is going through, to allow them tell their story and empathize with them. We need to physically be present and not run away when they are in their darkest hour. Jesus made this so clear when he took three with Him to be beside him in the garden of Gethsemane. Other times we often heard in Scriptures about Him going to a quiet place sometimes alone and sometimes with a few to pray. But He rebuked the disciples for this very sin of not being present at that dark hour. There were several reasons he rebuked them. He told them He did not want them tempted because He knew what they are facing and that prayer was essential for dealing with the temptation. But He also knew that there is strength in community and in spiritual prayer of agreement. If Jesus asked and sought others to walk alongside Him in Gesthemane and in day to day ministry and life shouldn't we likewise empathize with being there for church brothers and sisters in their darkest hours?

I can say as a minister and as a counselor that one of the biggest factors in people dying either from suicide or from health problems is whether people gather around them and hear their story and stand with them. Everyone needs someone to lift up their hands. No one can do it alone, no matter how spiritual they are. Jesus asked for that. We are likewise encouraged in the New Testament to bind together in community when one has needs- physical, emotional, etc. It is in the sense of Christian community that the suffering one can make the transition from the pain of a despairing soul to the hope of a living spirit. Fifty nine Scriptures about Christian community and being there for each other cannot be denied. Community and empathy with healthy communication are essential to living out the Gospel. Just a few examples of these are commands to "be at peace with each other" (Mark 9:50), "to love one another" (throughout John 13 & 15, Romans 13:8), to "honor each other above yourselves" (Romans 12:10), "to accept one another as Christ accepted you" (Romans 15:7), "to serve one another in love" (Galatians 5:13). With regard to the topic of being with each other in the darkest hour we are told to "carry each other's burdens" (Galatians 6:2), forgive each other" (Ephesians 4:32), to "submit to one another out of reverence for Christ" (Ephesians 5:21), and to "bear with one another in love" (Ephesians 4:2). We are warned against "devouring one another by being conceited and wanting our own ways and how this will only lead to destruction" (Galatians 5:15). If there is anything a true brother or sister in Christ should know how to do in the darkest hour it is to "speak in psalms, hymns, and spiritual songs" (Ephesians 5:19) and to "consider others as better than themselves" (Philippians 2:3). No one can deny that we are not meant to walk the road alone but with our brothers and sisters in Christ in community being readily available with Christian love, humility, encouragement, and edification lifting each other up. Just as we are grafted into the strength of the vine (Christ) we can likewise be grafted into the strengths of each other in the body of Christ.

Needless Hurt

Temptation Versus Suffering

Part of dealing with oppression and suicidal thoughts and feelings also involves having a realistic and sober spiritual mindset about temptation and suffering. In the New Testament Peter tells us to be sober minded about situations. We need to be realistic about what we are facing and put it in a proper spiritual context according to 1 Peter 5:8-11:

> Be sober, be vigilant; because your adversary the devil, as a roaring lion, walks about, seeking whom he may devour: Whom resist steadfast in the faith, knowing that the same afflictions are accomplished in your brethren that are in the world. But the God of all grace, who hath called us unto his eternal glory by Christ Jesus, after that ye have suffered a while, make you perfect, stablish, strengthen, settle you. To him be glory and dominion for ever and ever. Amen

Even if you consider yourself spiritually strong you should still be watchful and cautious. It is critical to remember that you are not alone in our suffering. This is one of the key lies the enemy will try and speak to your ears. There are as this Scripture suggests many around the world also facing various manner of suffering too.

It may seem natural to get into comparisons. Our issues are always worse (at least in our minds) than the next person's issues. We require immediate justice and correction for all our pain but we want God to be soft, gentle, and merciful towards us. We are special and should not, we reason, have to endure inconveniences. Because of the pain associated with our specific suffering we want to prioritize as if our suffering is really something magnificent compared to someone else's little trials. But all challenges and temptations and trials require us all to throw ourselves on Jesus's strength and mercy.

What does the Bible tell us about pain- temptations and suffering? The Greek word *peirasmos* is the word from which the words "trials" and "temptations" are taken in the Bible. The meaning of this word has to do with being under a test, a trial, or an experiment. It is akin to when someone is on a probationary period and the probation officer is watching to see how they react. However, there are some key differences between temptations and suffering which are important to notice.

Temptations are given by the devil to try and throw someone off their God given and determined course. They have to do with the enemy's plan to try and ensnare someone. Do you remember Jesus' temptation in the wilderness? He was about to embark on the beginning of His ministry. As a result he decided to get away to a remote place, a wilderness, to be readied for what lied ahead. This is exactly when they devil tried to take advantage of Jesus' weakened condition. He tried to get him to be distracted. He tried to get him to lust and negotiate for the kingdoms of the world. He tried to play on his natural need for food when fasting, encouraging Jesus to command stones to turn to bread.

The Bible tells us the details of this temptation in Matthew 4:1-11:

> Then was Jesus led up of the Spirit into the wilderness to be tempted of the devil. And when he had fasted forty days and forty nights, he was afterward and hungered. And when the tempter came to him, he said, If thou be the Son of God, command that these stones be made bread. But he answered and said, It is written, Man shall not live by bread alone, but by every word that proceeds out of the mouth of God. Then the devil took him up into the holy city, and set him on a pinnacle of the temple, and said unto him, If thou be the Son of God, cast thyself down: for it is written, He shall give his angels charge concerning thee: and in their hands they shall bear thee up, lest at any time thou dash thy foot against a stone. Jesus said unto him, It is written again, Thou shalt not tempt the Lord thy God. Again, the devil took him up into an exceeding high mountain, and showed him all the kingdoms of the world, and the glory of them; And said unto him, All these things will I give thee, if thou wilt fall down and worship me. Then said Jesus unto him, Get thee hence, Satan: for it is written, Thou shalt worship the Lord thy God, and him only shalt thou serve. Then the devil left him, and, behold, angels came and ministered unto him.

Let's look at some key principles in this passage from Matthew 4:1-11. First of all, whatever the devil says is always a twisted, distorted mess. The devil did not really care about Jesus being hungry and eating bread. He didn't care about Jesus having a nice ministry. The devil only was bent on the destruction and overthrow of the purposes for which Jesus became God in the flesh among us.

Likewise today the devil is bent on destruction of the purposes for which God created you. Maybe you think there are no great purposes for your life but the Bible tells us otherwise.

Note the devil's tactics. He tries to twist and manipulate some words and ideas. The manipulation always starts with some form of that "if you will...." The devil paints a glorious picture of everything that can be gained if only you will yield to compromise and do things his way. There is no "if" when we state Jesus is our Owner and Master and Lord of our life. Our response is only, "it is written." The Word of the Lord speaks for itself and does what it is purposed to do. No shortcuts, manipulations, Satanic deals, and negotiations will get us ever to the place the Lord has purposed for our lives quicker or easier.

We additionally must note Jesus' response to the devils twisting seen of Scripture. Jesus says, "It is written." If we do not know what is written in the Bible, what is God's authority on matters then we are trying to fight temptation with will power, logic, and other resources. The only thing that can shut up the devil is God's truth. James 4:7 tells us "Submit yourselves therefore to God. Resist the devil, and he will flee from you." But people argue- "he is not just going away. He still is bothering me."

What does the Biblical concept of resisting involve then? Resisting involves doing something different from what the devil wants you to do. So if he, for example, wants you to be distracted away from God's purposes then resisting means reading the Bible more, worshipping harder, and setting your eyes like flint before God. Make God "the Author and Finisher of your faith" (Hebrews 12:2) so that no temptation will throw you off course. Make His willingness to go to a brutal cross for you to be an Overcomer what you set your eyes on!

I cannot promise that the devil won't keep trying to see if he can throw you off course. This is his job. Remember he is "like a roaring lion seeking whom he may devour" from the earlier Scripture we read in 1 Peter. Notice that little but important key word "like". It does not say he *is* a roaring lion but rather he is *like* a roaring lion. So even in that he is a counterfeit. Through the roar he tries to create inconveniences and detours. He observes people's reactions to see how to respond. If we become upset and overtaken with temptation, stress, and traps then he has us. If we become consumed with the roar and fearing potential devouring then we are as good as dead. But if our ears are ears of faith guided by the Good Shepherd then the roar becomes like the squeak of a mouse and the voice of the Good Shepherd becomes louder than the devil's roar. 1 Corinthians 10:13 reminds us that "there hath no temptation taken you but such as is common to man: but God is faithful, who will not suffer you to be tempted above that ye are able; but will with the temptation also make a way to escape, that ye may be able to bear it."

Do you recall how many times you felt a warning in your conscience trying to get you to do otherwise then injure yourself or kill yourself? Do you recall how many times the doorbell rang, the phone rang, someone walked in, and your plans did not work? God was trying to provide a way out of suicide, out of the temptation to think you know a better end then the end he has for you. The thing is we need to perceive and see things accurately for what they are.

Temptation should be seen for what it is. James 1:14 defines temptation as each person being "lured and enticed by his own desire." More importantly, it is critical to know that there are Biblical solutions for dealing with temptation. According to Luke 22: 40 you can pray as a deterrent to giving into temptation. Jesus, for example, encouraged the disciples to do this before his death. We can also store up God's word in our hearts that we may not sin against him (Psalm 119:11) We can see temptation for what it is- an attempt to get us off course rather than anything the Lord has done to torture us or deprive us of the better things of life. For the Bible tells us to "let no one say when he is tempted, 'I am being tempted by God,' for God cannot be tempted with evil, and he himself tempts no one." (James 1:13) While temptations may be stressful to endure we must realize that we always have access to God's unlimited free gift of grace when we repent and change courses of our life.

Being tempted is something everyone faces including Jesus and the most holy seeming of church people. It is not the temptation itself that makes a person defeated but their reaction to it. Secular research has made some interesting discoveries about temptation as well that support this Biblical concept of needing to flee. Research shows that when someone who is tempted to overeat, fight someone, harm himself, or take any negative action for fifteen minutes actively runs toward and pursues an incompatible behavior the temptation loses its power.

For example, say you are in the sweets section of the grocery store and you are tempted to gorge on a cake when you get home. Don't stand staring and reflecting on the lovely assortments of cakes. Walk yourself and your cart as fast as you can to the fruit aisle and get some naturally healthy alternatives. Don't delay and debate about desserts. Don't reason and negotiate while you remain paralyzed by images of sweets.

If you have to even now make a list of alternative behaviors to whatever that areas you are tempted in. If it is eating wrong foods that is your downfall then plan menus, plan your shopping ahead. If it is wrong music choices stock up your i pod with worship music and program the hymns and praise songs. If it is relationships that are your downfall, plan for accountability friends who will keep you out in public and prevent you from being alone with more creeps and impulsive sexual situations.

Your reaction to temptations can be planned for. You may not always guess how and when temptations will occur but you can plan alternative behaviors which glorify God. And in fact, if you don't begin to make sure Biblically healthy behaviors are part of your day to day repertoire they will not be as natural when you really need to run to them to resist a temptation.

It is ridiculous to think that there is no need to plan ahead. If there is not an array of options your feelings will lead you to a decision which may feel gratifying in the moment but nonetheless brings long term hurt, deeper pain, and destruction. The good news then is that temptations do not have to your automatically lead to sin. You and I are not robots programmed to respond only to our feelings. However, if your brain is not exercised as any muscle your temptation overriding power will atrophy when most needed.

Do you recall how many times you felt a warning in your conscience trying to get you to do otherwise then injure yourself or kill yourself? Do you recall how many times the doorbell rang, the phone rang, someone walked in, and your plans did not work? God was trying to provide a way out of suicide, out of the temptation to think you know a better end then the end he has for you. The thing is we need to perceive and see things accurately for what they are.

Suffering and Trials

Now let's focus on suffering in general. Perhaps the biggest lie of all among Christian groups is that once you are a Christian life is easy, pleasant and does not involve any suffering. In case anyone has never told you I hope to give you the balanced and realistic perspective Scripture provides.

Too often the Bible talks about trials, crosses, and suffering. It talks about our faith being tested that we may develop the character and virtues of Christ and the fruit of the Spirit. Romans 5:3-5 states:

> but we glory in tribulations also: knowing that tribulation works patience; And patience, experience; and experience, hope: And hope makes not ashamed; because the love of God is shed abroad in our hearts by the Holy Ghost which is given unto us.

The attributes called the fruit of the Spirit listed in Galatians 5:22-23 which the Holy Spirit cultivates are: "love, joy, peace, forbearance, kindness, goodness, faithfulness, gentleness and self-control." They are not developed naturally or in the easy, good times. Who would be patient when they don't have to wait for something and trust for that? Who would have self-control when they naturally serve the lust for money, things, relationships, or habits that they believe temporarily make them feel good? Who would develop kindness and goodness unless pressed around by people who it is challenging to be kind to apart from the grace of God?

Suffering is a real part of life and is inescapable. This is why God wants you to learn to manage suffering. Otherwise he would not tell us that His grace is sufficient.

I cannot promise you in this life no tears or pain but I can promise you a God who is with you in the midst of suffering. The book of James tells us, "But let patience have her perfect work, that you may be perfect and entire, wanting nothing.

I can just imagine that you are thinking about how crazy it sounds to count sufferings as opportunities. But all too often we focus on the suffering rather than the long term outcome. We are like impulsive little kids who want the benefits of comfort, blessing, peace, and healing but without any waiting or obstacles. We want to be established in good things but the Bible makes it clear that God Himself will restore, confirm, strengthen, and establish only after we have endured the suffering. (1 Peter 5:10)

God never promises to take out the tribulations of this world but he promises that he has overcome the world's effects on us if we will yield to him (John 16:33). Going through sufferings of life is a small version of sharing in Christ's suffering. But we must not forget that this suffering paves the way for sharing in resurrection. 1 Peter 2:19-20 states that:

> this [suffering unjustly] is thankworthy, if a man for conscience toward God endure grief, suffering wrongfully...if, when you do well, and suffer for it, you take it patiently, this is acceptable with God.

*We are like impulsive little
kids who want the benefits
of comfort, blessing, peace,
and healing but without
any waiting or obstacles. We
want to be established in good
things but the Bible makes it
clear that God Himself will
restore, confirm, strengthen,
and establish only after we
have endured the suffering.
(1 Peter 5:10)*

Remember that you and I can only be revived if we already feel dead, drained, and at our wit's end.

It is fairy natural to think of sufferings as weights and burdens. We talk of being tied down. We talk of burdens that are unbearable. But rarely do we conceive of what the Bible calls "the weight of glory" once we have endured and shared with Christ in suffering unjustly (Romans 8:18). Now realistically the Bible does not suggest that we act in denial about unpleasant circumstances. For example, you may be pressed but we don't have to be crushed to where you don't get up. You may feel confused and not understand why God allows everything but you do not have to be forsaken. You may face persecution but you are not forsaken by God. You may feel struck down but it does not mean you need to stay in the mire and be destroyed by utter despair. You can be realistic about the toughness of life while also telling yourself the whole truth about how in spite of how life feels you have an unchangeable, consistent, and steadfast God (Hebrews 13:8).

How could someone like Paul who was imprisoned and beaten wrongfully endure? He definitely did not enjoy the suffering but he learned to rejoice in it. Let's note something here. I said you and I can by God's grace rejoice *in* suffering, not necessarily *because of* it. Rejoicing in suffering is not sadistically crying out for more pain but it is putting the pain in perspective. There may be afflictions but God always delivers us if we allow God to prove Himself according to Psalms 34:19:

> The eyes of the LORD are upon the righteous, and his ears are open unto their cry. The face of the LORD is against them that do evil, to cut off the remembrance of them from the earth. The righteous cry, and the LORD hears, and delivers them

out of all their troubles. The Lord is near unto them that are of a broken heart; and saves such as be of a contrite spirit. Many are the afflictions of the righteous: but the Lord delivers him out of them all. He keeps all his bones: not one of them is broken.

Psalm 22:24 likewise encourages us that "he hath not despised nor abhorred the affliction of the afflicted; neither hath he hid his face from him; but when he cried unto him, he heard.

You may wonder whether anything good can come out of trials and suffering. Did you ever notice how we read the Bible more and draw nearer to God when we have no other recourse? It is exactly like what Psalm 119:17 says: "we will obtain the crown of life by enduring to the end."

This is a point which is easily forgotten when life piles up. Suffering can never separate us from God. Never. Romans 8:35 reiterates this point: "Who shall separate us from the love of Christ? shall tribulation, or distress, or persecution, or famine, or nakedness, or peril, or sword?" The answer is a resounding "no one and nothing." Jesus loved us first before any trial. Jesus demonstrated for us how to "do suffering successfully" so he is not suggesting we do something of our own strength and abilities successfully. He can and will equip us to do successfully. To this end 1 Peter 2:19-21 states:

if when you do good and suffer for it you endure, this is a gracious thing in the sight of God. For to this you have been called, because Christ also suffered for you, leaving you an example, so that you might follow in his steps.

Jesus loved us first before any trial. Jesus demonstrated for us how to "do suffering successfully" so he is not suggesting we do something of our own strength and abilities successfully. He can and will equip us to do successfully.

Every circumstance whether deserved or undeserved is a tool in the hands of a perfect God. Remember this is the God who says you are "strong in Him and in the power of His might." (see Ephesians 4) Maybe you feel like you are a nothing in life. You feel like you live at the bottom of the barrel but to Him and in Him you are a royal priesthood. Maybe you feel like literally every area of your life has been touched by some tragedy from health to finances, to relationships, etc. This is the God who is like the Good Samaritan. When others pass by while you are "on the road in pain suffering" he stops to nurse your wounds, provide dose of reality and strength and take you to a heathier place.

Let's read the story of the Good Samaritan now from the Bible in Luke 10:25-37:

> And, behold, a certain lawyer stood up, and tempted him, saying, Master, what shall I do to inherit eternal life? He said unto him, What is written in the law? ...And he answering said, Thou shalt love the Lord thy God with all thy heart, and with all thy soul, and with all thy strength, and with all thy mind; and thy neighbor as thyself. And he said unto him, Thou hast answered right: this do, and thou shalt live. But he, willing to justify himself, said unto Jesus, And who is my neighbor? And Jesus answering said, A certain man went down from Jerusalem to Jericho, and fell among thieves, which stripped him of his raiment, and wounded him, and departed, leaving him half dead. And by chance there came down a certain priest that way: and when he saw him, he passed by on the other side. And likewise a Levite, when he was at the place, came and looked on him,

and passed by on the other side. But a certain Samaritan, as he journeyed, came where he was: and when he saw him, he had compassion on him, And went to him, and bound up his wounds, pouring in oil and wine, and set him on his own beast, and brought him to an inn, and took care of him. And on the morrow when he departed, he took out two pence, and gave them to the host, and said unto him, Take care of him; and whatsoever you spend more, when I come again, I will repay thee. Which now of these three was neighbor unto him that fell among the thieves? And he said, He that shewed mercy on him. Then said Jesus unto him, Go, and do thou likewise.

Notice the reactions of people. Maybe you have experienced one of these three patterns in your life. Maye you have people in your life who rob and strip you of your strength and your needs when you are at your weakest, lowest point. They think nothing of taking advantage of your vulnerability for their own gain as the robbers in this story did. Secondly, notice that even the priest passed by. Some people are too wrapped up in their own lives that they do not think of being there for someone else. It may even be in your situation that religious folk and church attendees passed by you the most. Maybe the ones who could have encouraged you and led you on the way and showed you Christ through their acts of mercy refused. They will have to answer to God for that.

I can assure you that if you are truly hungry and thirsty for a touch of God He will not pass you by. He will acknowledge your condition realistically. He will nurse you to health. He will bandage your broken heart for he is "near to the broken heart" (Psalm 34:18) and He "bottles all your tears." We are told He "keeps track of all our sorrows. He has collected all my tears in His bottle. He has recorded each one in His book." So if you ever wonder who knows what others have done to hurt you and the pain they have caused you God sure knows. He records it in a book it says. He holds our tears in a bottle (Psalm 56:8). He remembers what we have gone through and does not pass by those situations which have ailed us. He will put the oil of the presence of the Holy Spirit for strength outside yourself. He will anoint you with oil to break the oppression trying to hinder you from the life God intended for you. Then He will take you to a place of recovery though it may require some commitment from you to Him.

Let's take another example. Remember the woman at the well in John 4:1-26. She had many husbands and the man she was with at the time Jesus encountered her was not even her current husband. She had many sources to try and feel good about herself. Eventually even the relationships could not do that anymore. Maybe you have impulsively gotten into one relationship after another. There is a well that will keep you thrilled and give you hope and energy and sustenance more than any sweet words of your earthly liver ever can. He is Jesus.

So why do I bring up temptation and suffering? It is because those are some of the very reasons I hear people state for wanting to commit suicide. Temptation and suffering will happen but you can face it. You are not alone as the voice in your mind tells you. The Bible tells us we are more effective and powerful in Christ than any devil (1 John 4:4). This means that we are glued to Jesus. We are like a Siameze twin connected to Him when we surrender out lives to Him. We who are weak and weary and worn are glued to life, hope, energy, and unending source. John 15:4-7 puts it this way:

> Abide in me, and I in you. As the branch cannot bear fruit of itself, except it abide in the vine; no more can ye, except ye abide in me. I am the vine, ye are the branches: He that abides in me, and I in him, the same brings forth much fruit: for without me ye can do nothing. If a man abide not in me, he is cast forth as a branch, and is withered; and men gather them, and cast them into the fire, and they are burned. If ye abide in me, and my words abide in you, ye shall ask what ye will, and it shall be done unto you.

The Bible says "there is hope yet for a tree" in Job 14:7. When a tree is cut to a stump most people fail to see its beauty. But the point is even when the leaves are cut down and it is not as high and majestic as it used to be it has hope. It can still grow even with only a stump. Today you may feel like nothing's left of you but a stump. But that's where God can say "good, let's grow something beautiful from the little you have left." What testimony would it be to God's greatness if you and I were already great on our own? The testimony is that God chooses "the foolish things to confound the wise." (1 Corinthians 1:27) He chooses to put the treasure of His presence and victory in earthern vessels- in you and me! (2 Corinthians 4:7). He chooses the worthless paining stumps to grow His glory. He chooses the ones who tried many wrong things in the past and failed. He chooses the ones who feel forgotten and left by the side of the road as in the Good Samaritan story.

Today He chooses you. In case no one ever told you. Know now that He chooses you. He says in His strength you are not too far gone. Whatever temptations and trials and suffering have come or whatever will come He is willing to partner with you if you'll lean on Him. How will you respond today? Will you turn away because the suffering is too hard or inconvenient or will you turn to the one who masters the suffering and is resurrection Himself?

He called the one who endures for righteousness sake the inconveniences, the pains, the persecutions, the betrayals "blessed." (Matthew 5:1-12) He never said it feels blessed. But the word *blessed* means favored. Only those who go through the sufferings can we see the fullness of the majesty and power, the authority and victory of a God who is very much alive today.

May we be like Job who in spite of losing everything he loved naturally in the world still held fast to his integrity (Job 2:3-7). The secret, brother Paul tells us, is to confess, believe, and act on the belief "in all circumstances I can do all things through Christ who strengthens me." (Philippians 4:12-14). Of ourselves we will not have strength all the time. We can't do all things. It will surely feel like there is too much to handle. But there is even now if you will allow it a grand opportunity for the strength of the God of the heavens to rise up within you. He can give you motivation when you feel unmotivated, joy when you have endless tears, perspective when your eyes have been blinded. It is not too much for the God who conquered Calvary to overcome in and through you what you are facing today.

Today you may feel like nothing's left of you but a stump. But that's where God can say "good, let's grow something beautiful from the little you have left." What testimony would it be to God's greatness if you and I were already great on our own? The testimony is that God chooses "the foolish things to confound the wise." (1 Corinthians 1:27) He chooses to put the treasure of His presence and victory in earthern vessels- in you and me! (2 Corinthians 4:7). He chooses the worthless paining stumps to grow His glory. He chooses the ones who tried many wrong things in the past and failed. He chooses the ones who feel forgotten and left by the side of the road as in the Good Samaritan story.

We fear the unknown. But what if God has been to our future? What if God is really for us and His purposes in our lives? If He is for us then nothing- absolutely nothing- can be so against us that we have no option but suicide. Romans 8:31-32 says:

> What shall we then say to these things? If God be for us, who can be against us? He that spared not his own Son, but delivered him up for us all, how shall he not with him also freely give us all things?

Therefore, let us cling to Ephesians 6:10-18 as we move forward in the strength of the living God:

> Finally, my brethren, be strong in the Lord, and in the power of his might. Put on the whole armor of God, that ye may be able to stand against the wiles of the devil. For we wrestle not against flesh and blood, but against principalities, against powers, against the rulers of the darkness of this world, against spiritual wickedness in high places. Wherefore take unto you the whole armor of God, that ye may be able to withstand in the evil day, and having done all, to stand. Stand therefore, having your loins girt about with truth, and having on the breastplate of righteousness; And your feet shod with the preparation of the gospel of peace; Above all, taking the shield of faith, wherewith ye shall be able to quench all the fiery darts of the wicked. And take the helmet of salvation, and the sword of the Spirit, which is the word of God: Praying always with all prayer and supplication in the Spirit, and watching thereunto with all perseverance and supplication for all saints.

Three Voices During Pain: God, The Enemy, and Self

There are three different types of voices that can manage how we approach life. These are not necessarily audible voices but are inner inclinations we lean to. The first voice for those who are Christians is that of God through a relationship with Jesus Christ, the Savior. The second voice which can be prominent during times of temptation, oppression, or utter despair which speaks negativity and suicide is that of the enemy (devil) and powers and principalities of darkness. The third voice is that of our own inner thoughts from the emotions connected to our life experiences. This is called the fleshly or carnal man.

The Voice of God

Let's start by first talking about the voice of God. The voice of God for someone should be pertinent, relevant, and meaningful for someone who knows and walks with Him. This means that if you, for example, call yourself a Christian you should sense the voice of God through the Bible and times of fellowship with Him. For the purposes of this book let's be clear that a Christian is not merely someone who takes membership at a church, is on a committee or board, or does good deeds. A Christian is not something which can be earned by virtue of one's family lineage (e.g. "because my grandma prayed and my dad was a deacon"). It is a life of surrender to the personhood of Jesus Christ. The Bible tells us in Romans 10:9-13 that we must confess Jesus Christ as Lord, repent of sin, and be baptized.

Confession is not just a rote repeated prayer acting a checklist to make it into heaven. It is a heartfelt cry from deep within that says, "I can't do this life alone. Even at my best I am miserable and helpless." Even when things have happened to go well it is less because of who I am and more because of all God is. It is God who "judges the thoughts and intents of the heart" (1 Samuel 16:7, Proverbs 15:11, Hebrews 4:12). So thus, salvation is about a condition of being and relating rather than simply outward actions.

Repentance is also another part of the Christian walk. If there is something which is not consistent with a life God approves of Biblically repentance involves turning away from that behavior. This turning away is first having a mindset in agreement with God that things He disapproves of have no place in our lives. Then, secondly, repentance involves choosing to walk in new actions which line up with Godly lifestyle.

The struggle for many of us involves trying to do this walk through our own determined self-will. The strongest most self-willed person cannot possibly succeed at every area of life on his or her own. And any apparent "success" is only because of God's grace. This is where the depression and suicidal thoughts or behaviors can come in. They are rooted in the belief that "I can ever handle any stress, anxiety, depression, life problems, physical pain, or impossible feeling situations with my strength."

In the Bible Jesus at times even needed to be encouraged by the angels (Matthew 4:1-11). He had a team of twelve around him and made use of social and ministry supports and accountability. It was His submitting Himself to His Father's Will that gave Him strength, not because he was a strong determined self-willed person.

This submission to God's voice modeled by Jesus in John 13:1-17 should serve as an example to us:

> Jesus knowing that the Father had given all things into his hands, and that he was come from God, and went to God; He arose from supper, and laid aside his garments; and took a towel, and girded himself. After that he poured water into a basin, and began to wash the disciples' feet, and to wipe them with the towel wherewith he was girded. Then cometh he to Simon Peter: and Peter said unto him, Lord, dost thou wash my feet? Jesus answered and said unto him, What I do thou know not now; but thou shalt know hereafter. Peter said unto him, Thou shalt never wash my feet. Jesus answered him, If I wash thee not, thou hast no part with me. Simon Peter said unto him, Lord, not my feet only, but also my hands and my head. Jesus said to him, He that is washed needs not save to wash his feet, but is clean every whit: and ye are clean, but not all. For he knew who should betray him; therefore said he, Ye are not all clean. So after he had washed their feet, and had taken his garments, and was set down again, he said unto them, Know ye what I have done to you? Ye call me Master and Lord: and ye say

well; for so I am. If I then, your Lord and Master, have washed your feet; ye also ought to wash one another's feet. For I have given you an example, that ye should do as I have done to you. Verily, verily, I say unto you, The servant is not greater than his lord; neither he that is sent greater than he that sent him.

We are told that God's sheep "hear and know His voice" (see John 10:27). Again, this does not mean those who just say they "believe in God" or that God exists but rather is those who make hanging out with God a priority similar to hanging out with a best friend.

Think about it. You don't become someone's best friend overnight. Even if the two of you "click" right away you generally do not share the most intimate of all things the first few times you meet. It is like this with our walk with God. It takes us time to get to know him and become accustomed with Him to where His voice becomes more familiar and can be distinguished from other voices. Also it takes time to go from just knowing about God as a distant man in the heavens to relating to Him as a personal relational God who cares about details of your everyday life. Psalm 100:3 also tells us, "Know ye that the LORD he is God: it is he that hath made us, and not we ourselves; we are his people, and the sheep of his pasture."

The other subsequent piece which Scripture speaks of is that once someone hears the voice of God and recognizes it they should follow that voice. It is one thing for you or I to know what to do but it is a whole other thing to do it. For example, it is one thing to know that God says he desires to give you "a future and a hope" (see Jeremiah 29:11-13) and "an abundant life" (John 10:10) but another thing doubting this and planning suicidal ways to escape from life's pain.

It boils down to each of us individually answering the question, "do I really believe what God says about my life?" Do I really deep down think that He does know what He is talking about? Notice I said "do I believe it?" NOT "do I agree with it or feel it?" When the storms of life rage around you it is not natural to feel the anticipation of abundant life coming. When one trial and temptation after another comes it is easy for our natural emotions to be stirred up or be as the psalmist described as being "disquieted" or uneasy."

It boils down to each of us individually answering the question, "do I really believe what God says about my life?" Do I really deep down think that He does know what He is talking about?

In fact, hearing and doing God's word by His grace alone is the key way of identifying who is "of God." (see John 8:47). There is blessing even in the difficulty to keeping God's word (Luke 11:28). Perhaps the greatest blessing is the comfort of the Holy Spirit. The comforter, the Holy Spirit , Jesus, tells us will teach us all things and bring that which Jesus said to our remembrance (John 14:26) The problem is sometimes we are so busy dwelling on the stresses of life that seem to preoccupy us so easily that we don't even want an alternative to be brought to our remembrance.

Did you know that this is like saying, "God, leave me to wallow in self-pity. I want my pain. I do not want to be comforted. I want the right to complain. I want the attention from others. I deserve the right to speak because of what I have gone through. Now there is some level of truth to this but there is also another sobering truth to add to this. Jesus dies a death He absolutely did not deserve. He was led "as a lamb to the slaughter" (Isaiah 53:7) to a brutal death yet instead of arguing and fighting back He allowed His Father's truth to prevail and the Father's purposes to win out. Scripture tells us in Isaiah 53:7, "He was oppressed, and he was afflicted, yet he opened not his mouth; like a lamb that is led to the slaughter, and like a sheep that before its shearers is silent, so he opened not his mouth." In Gesthemane though he was real in crying out, "can you please take this up (of pain) from me?" He yet responded, "not my will but thine be done."

Our will in times of excruciating pain is certainly to escape. Our will is to have things over and done with. Our will is to give up. Our will is to let someone else bear the burden we feel we have been bearing for so long. Our will is to make the other persons who have wronged us pay by having to suffer the rest of their lives. Our will is to do anything but stand and watch God be God.

It is so illogical isn't it? The Bible tells us to stand. You may naturally think, "but I have done everything I know to do." That is exactly the point the Bible makes as well when it says "having done all to stand" (Ephesians 6:13). You probably have exhausted your personal strength, spent your money, depleted your resources, reduced your options. But the God who takes care of the lilies of the field with water from the sky and nutrients and feeds the birds of the air with worms in all the right places also provides for us in ways we cannot fathom. Listen to Matthew 6:25-34:

> Therefore I say unto you, Take no thought for your life, what ye shall eat, or what ye shall drink; nor yet for your body, what ye shall put on. Is not the life more than meat, and the body than raiment? Behold the fowls of the air: for they sow not, neither do they reap, nor gather into barns; yet your heavenly Father feeds them. Are ye not much better than they? Which of you by taking thought can add one cubit unto his stature? And why take ye thought for raiment? Consider the lilies of the field, how they grow; they toil not, neither do they spin: And yet I say unto you, That even Solomon in all his glory was not arrayed like one of these. Wherefore, if God so clothe the grass of the field, which today is, and tomorrow is cast into the oven, shall he not much more clothe you, O ye of little faith? Therefore take no thought, saying, What shall we eat? or, What shall we drink? or, Wherewithal shall we be clothed? For after all these things do the Gentiles seek for

> your heavenly Father knows that ye have need of all these things. But seek ye first the kingdom of God, and his righteousness; and all these things shall be added unto you. Take therefore no thought for the morrow: for the morrow shall take thought for the things of itself. Sufficient unto the day is the evil thereof.

So one voice we have to cultivate hearing, receiving, and following if we are to overcome the voice of suicide and premature death is that of God's voice. No faith and life will come to you but by this. Romans 10:17 says that "faith comes by hearing and hearing by the Word of God." Repeating mantras and motivational sayings will not motivate you enough to stay alive if you are at your wit's end. Considering everyone's opinions around you will only confuse you more. Spending all your money on doctors and exhausting your resources will only leave you depleted and dry.

So being told that God's sheep know His voice, hear His voice and listen to or obey His voice we must then understand what it is to be God's sheep.

Sheep are naturally stubborn in that they like to wander. They have their own inclinations and sometimes can be rather slow to get things. However, throughout Scripture we are told that we have a God who is patient and longsuffering with us. He desires that none should miss eternal life (2 Peter 3:9). Even in the parable of the lost sheep He talks about how if you even were the one lost sheep He as the Good Shepherd (John 10:11) would forsake the ninety nine to come for you. All your wanderings cannot keep him from pursuing you according to Luke 15: 4-7:

What man of you, having an hundred sheep, if he lose one of them, doth not leave the ninety and nine in the wilderness, and go after that which is lost, until he find it? And when he hath found it, he lays it on his shoulders, rejoicing. And when he comes home, he calls together his friends and neighbors, saying unto them, Rejoice with me; for I have found my sheep which was lost. I say unto you, that likewise joy shall be in heaven over one sinner that repents, more than over ninety and nine just persons, which need no repentance.

Another Scripture which brings this idea home is Psalm 139:7-12:

Where can I go from your Spirit?
    Where can I flee from your presence?
If I go up to the heavens, you are there;
    if I make my bed in the depths, you are there.
If I rise on the wings of the dawn,
    if I settle on the far side of the sea,
even there your hand will guide me,
    your right hand will hold me fast.
If I say, "Surely the darkness will hide me
    and the light become night around me,"
even the darkness will not be dark to you;
    the night will shine like the day,
    for darkness is as light to you

Notice that this passage says the phrase "even if I make my bed even in hell." God's love is always reaching out. Perhaps today you feel like you have wandered to the farthest and most undesirable places in your life. You have hung with some of the biggest low lifes. You have made decisions you wished you hadn't made and suffered regrets a mile high. You feel like you are already living in hell. God has not given up on you yet for some reason. You may not understand why yet. People around you may not understand why yet either. But He knows exactly how all you are fit into His plan. He can turn your worst mess around if you will allow Him to reach into your hell with His love now.

One of the biggest lies of the devil is that your life is just too far gone. You have made too many mistakes and sinned too much that even God has to turn His back on you. Then Paul would never have been the great apostle he was. Who would have believed in a mass murderer like Paul? Not anyone. But God did so much so that he met him on the road to Damascus and personally gave Him an encounter to show him how much He cared and saw a different life for him (Acts chapter 9). What about the thief on the cross next to Jesus? He was a criminal for sure. He deserved the punishment for a crime. He had no time to take a church membership, do some good deeds, or follow any religious rituals. Yet due to his sincere heart Jesus said, "you will be with me this day in paradise." (Luke 23:43)

Sheep also take time to comprehend things. Maybe you tried church or God before and it did not seem to work. Maybe sadly some people misrepresented God and turned you off. People are not God. They can do a miserable job of representing Him. Would you consider asking God in your own humble way to show himself to you? Grieve the ways you have not known or understood him. Grieve the wounds you have. Allow Him to be what people can never be for you.

If we are to be as sheep we need to be aware of some key principles:

1. **The life of the sheep is of genuine and personal interest to the Shepherd**. The sheep lived among that shepherd like a young infant child dependent on his mother or father. Sheep can differentiate between the loyal, protective one who cares for it and the ones who do not care.

2. **Sheep do not take matters into their own hands**. In fact in the natural sheep are not made with the type of horns that can really injure anything. The ones who have horns only have rounded horns which can barely do any damage. A sheep will likely stand still and be defenseless when predators come if it does not have the defense and protection of the shepherd.

3. **Sheep become discouraged and will even allow themselves who die when wilderness experiences happen**. If the sun is hot and the land is dry, sheep will not go to water. Sheep do not naturally go to the place of life and hope and strength. Instead, they stand in the hot sun while their own bodies and the land around them are parched. Unless sheep are "led beside still waters" (see Psalm 23:1-6) they will die. Likewise, unless we admit our utter weakness and allow ourselves to be led beside still waters we will surely die. We will only see suicide as an option.

The alternative to the traditional stubbornness of sheep is the only thing that brings lasting refreshing, renewed life and hope. This resting and assurance is described as follows:

The LORD is my shepherd; I shall not want. He makes me to lie down in green pastures: he leads me beside the still waters. He restores my soul: he leads me in the paths of righteousness for his name's sake. Yea, though I walk through the valley of the shadow of death, I will fear no evil: for thou art with me; thy rod and thy staff they comfort me. You prepare a table before me in the presence of mine enemies: you anoint my head with oil; my cup runs over. Surely goodness and mercy shall follow me all the days of my life: and I will dwell in the house of the LORD forever.

One of the biggest lies of the devil is that your life is just too far gone. You have made too many mistakes and sinned too much that even God has to turn His back on you. Then Paul would never have been the great apostle he was. Who would have believed in a mass murderer like Paul? Not anyone. But God did so much so that he met him on the road to Damascus and personally gave Him an encounter to show him how much He cared and saw a different life for him.

Without relying on God's shepherding people will come to the conclusion "I have no way out." All they feel is the scorching sun. All they see is the dryness. They need to be led. It may be simple as starting to pick up a Bible today that you through on a shelf years ago because you were made at God and beginning to read it again. It may be simple as attending a good Bible believing church when you have felt burned by people because no one was there for you in the past. It may be putting on some hymns and worship music when you feel no song in your heart and would rather call your friend to talk trash and complain.

Will you let yourself be led to the water? Will you let God do for you what you cannot do yourself?

Another noteworthy issue we see in the Bible is that sheep are compared to goats. There will always be frauds and counterfeits. Goats can look like sheep but their chromosomes and genetic makeup are entirely different. Goats like a rocky mountainous ground. They like trying to stubbornly do things on their own. They will ram a situation with their horns when faced with trouble rather than waiting to be led to the still waters. Goats eat high up lives and refuse to bow their heads in humility to eat the lower grasses which sheep eat. As a result, goats end up more prone to parasites and fight to build up the immunity which sheep have.

The Bible says, "If today you hear His voice harden not your heart." (Hebrews 3:15) All too often we reach a point were God is trying to speak but we do not listen. Why not give Him a chance today? What do you have to lose?

Did you know that those things you are so preoccupied and on pain about are the very ones He has already taken on Himself. That is the very pain He bore when his entrails hung out of His body and his face and body were marred beyond recognition. Why bear what he already bore? You can't do it. I can't do it. We are not little Gods. We were never designed to carry so much.

Have you heard the Scripture "His yoke is easy and His burden light?" (Matthew 11:28-30). Did you ever wonder what this Scripture meant? When oxen are wearing a yoke around their necks to plow a weaker ox is always linked with a more experienced one. It is the same in our walk in life. We are the less experienced "ox." God is the much more experienced one. He has plowed the ground of your issues before. He has seen into your current pains and sees His ability in you to overcome. Why act then act as if you are trying to tell Him a thing or two? You and I are and never will be the more experienced ones. We will never be able to guide the plow and take him along for a ride. But that's what we do when we contemplate suicide and attempt it. We are saying, "I've chosen this. I know better."

I don't know of anyone who feels utter despair that would not long for a lighter, easier yoke. I don't know of anyone whose heart is ridden with pain that would not like for the oil of gladness to be poured on their hearts.

*We are the less experienced
"ox." God is the much more
experienced one. He has plowed
the ground of your issues before.
He has seen into your current
pains and sees His ability in
you to overcome. Why act then
act as if you are trying to tell
Him a thing or two? You and
I are and never will be the
more experienced ones. We will
never be able to guide the plow
and take him along for a ride.
But that's what we do when
we contemplate suicide and
attempt it. We are saying, "I've
chosen this. I know better."*

The Voice of The Enemy

The second voice which can be in play is the voice of the devil or his powers and principalities of darkness. Again it is not usually an audible voice but in some cases people may become so oppressed that they even hear command hallucinations telling them how awful they are, how they need to end their life.

The devil always speaks a part truth, a half-truth, or a distortion of truth. In other cases he only speaks lies. That's another reason why it is so important to know what the Bible says. We just read about how the sheep of the Lord know His voice. In John 10:1-9 we read:

> He that enters not by the door into the sheep-fold, but climbs up some other way, the same is a thief and a robber. But he that enters in by the door is the shepherd of the sheep. To him the porter opens; and the sheep hear his voice: and he calls his own sheep by name, and leads them out. And when he puts forth his own sheep, he goes before them, and the sheep follow him: for they know his voice. And a stranger will they not follow, but will flee from him: for they know not the voice of strangers.

So we must know how to distinguish the voice of the enemy then. There are several ways the enemy may try and "speak" to us. Remember that these may not be an audible voice but an idea that comes in your mind or through a person, situation, media, or venue which tries to get you to do something other than what is God's plan for your life.

The list below are just some of the most common tactics the enemy uses:

Tactic #1: He speaks things or ideas which are contrary to Biblical principles.

Example: For example, he may tell you that "God just wants you to feel good and have fun in life all the time and to never feel unhappy or uncomfortable."

Truth: We know this is not true because God wants us to have abundant eternal life in Jesus Christ but never promises that life will be uneasy or without trials and discomfort. Jesus is our example and He went through a lot of trials, discomfort, and hurts and pains yet chose to rely on the assistance of the Holy Spirit to get him through.

Tactic #2: He gets you to exalt your own feelings above the spiritual state of your soul being in line with what a soul renewed in Christ would do.

Example: He will give you an excuse to kill yourself, take drugs, or have promiscuous sex because you feel awful.

Truth: A Biblical alterative would be to acknowledge the discomfort but still feed your spirit man with Scriptures about alternative choices and the joy of finding fulfillment in the Lord. For example, you could feed yourself with Scripture like "in God's presence is fullness of joy and at His right hand are pleasures forevermore." (Psalm 16:11)

Tactic #3: He observes where you are weak and what pushes your buttons and then keeps pushing the same buttons to keep you weak, vulnerable, and inclining to sin.

Example: When things are rough at work or your kids argue and disobey he sees your reactions and hopelessness. He knows these are button pushers for you so he tries to get you to pay an extraordinary amount of time to these button pushers rather than what is spiritually true.

Truth: You can remind yourself of the Bible truth which counteracts the button pushers. If you cannot think of it yourself then you should consider talking with someone who is not also in a rut who can give you a sense of realistic perspective and healthy optimism.

The devil always mixes a part truth and part lie to create a distortion that sounds appealing. For example he may say, "God ideally wants you to not have sex outside of marriage but he really knows you are weak and you are tempted so he understands if you fall." He doesn't tell you about God's strength beyond your own or God's sufficient grace to deliver you in the moment. He doesn't tell you about the consequences of the short term pleasure of suiting your own desires. He only stresses the inconvenience to you and then puts a spin on things like "God surely would not want you to be inconvenienced, would he?" It is the same lie the serpent told Eve in Genesis: "God really certainly did not mean that, did he?"

It does not do much good to only be able to recognize the voice of the enemy if we cannot do something about it. We can choose to not listen to this voice. We can see it for the lies it is. We can renew our mind with Scriptural truths. We can believe the truth that "greater is he within us than the enemy" (1 John 4:4). We can choose to believe that nothing- not life stresses, devils, or things which seem beyond us- can ever separate us from the Lord's Will for us. Romans 8:37-39 says:

> Nay, in <u>all</u> these things, we are more than con-
> querors through Him that loved us. For I am per-
> suaded that neither death, nor life, nor angels,
> nor principalities, nor powers, nor height, nor
> depth, nor any other creature, shall be able to
> separate us from the love of God, which is in
> Christ Jesus our Lord.

The Voice of Self and Flesh

The third voice is that of self or flesh. Before we can understand this we must understand the way we are made. We have a spirit man which for the Christian is surrendered to the Lord Jesus Christ. We live in a body with physical aches and pains, and needs. We also have an intellect which reasons and receives things rationally. We have emotions which respond to our desires for things. The intellect, will, and emotions all become parts of the soul which may or may not line up with things spiritually.

Sometimes when we have faced so many wounds or so much stress in life it is easy to let events take on a life of their own. For example, the person who was molested as a child and then raped as a young adult may consider herself an object and may never believe she is able to be properly loved and respected. The person whose chronic physical pain makes mobility difficult may think about how all his or her relatives died young and may become discouraged about starting new healthy weight loss and eating habits. The person who struggles with an addiction may feel so bound that all he can see is another day of barely getting by.

If you and I do not allow the Holy Spirit to teach and take over, rule, and reign in the body the natural inclinations are for the fleshly carnal man to take over. You or I can become fleshy or carnal if our appetites are rooted in self. How do we know what falls under this category of flesh or carnality? 1 Timothy 6:3-5 gives some good examples:

> If any man teach otherwise, and consent not to wholesome words, even the words of our Lord Jesus Christ, and to the doctrine which is according to godliness; He is proud, knowing nothing, but doting about questions and strifes of words, whereof comes envy, strife, railings, evil surmisings, perverse disputings of men of corrupt minds, and destitute of the truth, supposing that gain is godliness: from such withdraw thyself.

Another example of being in the flesh or carnal is when you say you are a "Christian" yet you still are as a babe in Christ. There is no growth or maturity. You allow no Scriptural challenges to mature you onto Him. You thrive on remaining ignorant and behaving in a human way rather than a spiritually guided way. (1 Corinthians 3:1-23) Additionally, the natural person "does not accept and disregards the spiritual things." (1 Corinthians 2:14) For example we see a tendency in an effort to be politically correct and people pleasing for so many even within churches to allow some pieces of the Bible mixed in with some worldliness, mixed with what is popular among attendees personal beliefs rather than the foundation being 100% upon the immovable unshakeable rock of Jesus Christ as Cornerstone.

When this happens there is a definite distinction that over time becomes apparent. Romans 8:5-8 puts it this way:

> For to set the mind on the flesh is death, but to set the mind on the spirit is life and peace. For the mind that is set on the flesh is hostile to God for it does not submit to God's law; indeed it cannot. Those in the flesh cannot please God.

In Scripture we are commanded to choose either life or death. You cannot have life and death co-occurring. Yet this is what those who walk in carnality and flesh try to do. They say "yes- I'm a Christian" but they mix all sorts of beliefs to a melting pot of death which brings no eternal life whatsoever. This cannot please God according to the Bible.

The only way God will be pleased and our lives will be the closet to what God purposed for them in the first place is to choose what is life-giving. Do you know that what is good is not always pleasant? A young child may find it adventuresome to run across the road to the ice cream shop while cars are coming at him yet it is surely not in his best interest. A lonely person may find it momentarily comforting to find empty hugs in the arms of strangers who wisper flattery she never had growing up. A young man may find temporary happiness with an emotional high after smoking and snorting drugs because no one introduced him to the joy of the Lord which is a constant ever-flowing unshakeable knowledge of the

peace and assurance of heaven's resources at your door-
step in the person of Jesus Christ walking alongside you
in all circumstances.

The natural man does not receive the things of the
Spirit of God for they are foolishness to him and "are spiritually discerned" (1 Corinthians 2:14) Because he does not
allow himself to be led of the Lord's Spirit which leads to
authentic conversion and newness he ends up "fulfilling
the lusts of the flesh and becoming a child or wrath."
(Ephesians 2:3)

Let's use an analogy in the natural world. Do you have
favorite foods you like to feed on? If you feed on what is
immediately good you may eat chocolate, sugar, sweet
things, and what your cravings desire. But if you learn to
walk in a healthy way you develop a taste and even a liking
for fruits and vegetables and balanced meals. It is similar
spiritually. Our carnal man does not naturally automatically incline towards fruits and vegetables but inclines
towards the immediate deceptive short-lived sweetness
of sin. The inclination only becomes preoccupied with the
satisfaction of the moment but never tells you about the
cavities you will develop, the stomach problems that will
happen, the destruction to your digestive tract.

While the appetites of sin and the flesh may start out
seeming attractive I can assure you in the years of counseling practice I have seen so many who eventually said
"now I can't stop." They report how a one time fleshly
carnal pleasure in a few weeks or months overtook them
to a path they cannot get out of without the intervention
of the Holy Spirit.

The good news is that there is the alternative of
walking in the Spirit. No man including the most charis-
matic preacher can draw you long enough or convincingly
enough if the Holy Spirit does not lead you to God. Only

the Holy Spirit can convince you and me of our own insufficiency and His all sufficiency.

You may be the one who has attempted or contemplated suicide or you may have gone through an emotional suicide. Whatever the story there is none of us who can survive this stressful world on our own sufficiency. No amount of money, friends, favor, or things will give permanent happiness. The Bible puts it this way: "For all (on their own) have fallen short of the Glory of God. All of our righteousness is as filthy rags." (Romans 3:23)

Here's the good news. Today can be the day you bring your filthy rags to the altar of the foot of the cross of Jesus Christ. You can stop holding the filthy rags, caressing them, talking about them, and making them into gods. You can stop believing there is no way out of the mire and filth.

If you remember one thing from this book I hope you lay hold of the fact that there are alternative choices in your life. There is an alternative way of reacting to hopelessness which does not add more filth. The alternative can begin today. You cannot defeat suicidal thoughts and behaviors with a one time pep talk and Bible verse. You must cultivate a lifestyle which reteaches yourself to think, feel, and behave as governed by the Holy Spirit rather than the flesh. This means that you choose to listen to and follow the voice of the Good Shepherd ultimately over the voices of your own perceptions, experiences, or the devil.

Walking in the spirit as defined by Ephesians 4:1 involves

> walking worthy of the vocation wherewith ye are called, with all lowliness and meekness, with longsuffering, forbearing one another in love; Endeavoring to keep the unity of the Spirit in the bond of peace.

The mind is either focused on being preoccupied with things of the flesh or things of the spirit in this walk (Romans 8:1-39) The Bible is clear about the division between flesh and Spirit: "Anyone who does not have the Spirit of God does not belong to Him." (Romans 8:9)

Maybe you have never known you belong – really, really belong to anybody or anything except hurt, pain, abuse trauma, and rejection. But today you can belong to Jesus. You can belong to new hope. You can belong to the one who is the resurrection beyond the immeasurable hurts in your life. You can belong to Him. You can enter into His rest, his comfort. He will ask you to leave the filthy rags at His cross. They may be outward sins like murder, abuse, rage, ager, hate, jealousy, fornication, gluttony or they may be inward sins like wrong attitudes, bitterness, unforgiveness, inner beliefs that do not glorify God. You don't have to be married to those things.

Maybe you have never known you belong – really, really belong to anybody or anything except hurt, pain, abuse trauma, and rejection. But today you can belong to Jesus. You can belong to new hope. You can belong to the one who is the resurrection beyond the immeasurable hurts in your life. You can belong to Him. You can enter into His rest, his comfort.

Someone wants you. If you've ever felt kicked to the curb, as if you do not fit in, unloved, and given up on someone wants you today. If you ever felt disgusted by yourself as if you had to give up on yourself because you are not who you wanted to be, someone wants you. He will hug you. He will receive you. He will embrace you and he will shape you if you will continue choosing to walk in the Holy Spirit that is drawing you even now.

You are wanted. Will you receive? Will you accept the walk with the Holy Spirit? Will you stop looking at and being encumbered by the sin at present and behind? Will you instead take steps ahead to the victory of walking with the healer, deliverer and strength you need in the best friendship you have ever known? Maybe this is going to be the first real best friend you've ever known. Maybe this is the first time you will let someone really wisper God's truth to your heart. It's not too late.

Hear the knock at the door of your heart. It is Jesus Christ through the drawing of the Holy Spirit. Will you allow me in? Can I be the authentic one you were looking for in all the wrong places? Can I strengthen you to walk in the right place? Can I shape and mold you into someone you never thought you can be? It may take time but I promise you you will never be alone. I say to you reading this book just like I said to the disciples, "I will never leave nor forsake you." Will you open the door and receive me?

Someone wants you. If you've ever felt kicked to the curb, as if you do not fit in, unloved, and given up on someone wants you today. If you ever felt disgusted by yourself as if you had to give up on yourself because you are not who you wanted to be, someone wants you. He will hug you. He will receive you. He will embrace you and he will shape you if you will continue choosing to walk in the Holy Spirit that is drawing you even now.

Overcoming Preoccupation With Negativity

D oes God really care about me?
It can be very easy to believe the lie that because you are going through things maybe God is not there at all or that if He is somewhere He is a distant, uncaring entity who is not concerned about what you go through. However, the Bible tells us in the book of Hebrews that we have a High Priest who is familiar with what he have or are going through. Hebrews 4:15 mentions that "we have not an high priest which cannot be touched with the feeling of our infirmities; but was in all points tempted like as we are, yet without sin." For example, he under-stood grief and lost when his best friend Lazarus died. He understood righteous anger when the religious leaders distorted the message of the Gospel. He understood the needs of people and was moved with compassion when crowds of people were without food such that He mul-tiplied some bread and fish so they could eat. He knew the pain of betrayal as He anticipated one of His twelve who He lived with and associated with day by day turning him over to be killed. He knew utter betrayal in looking

across the crowds to those he had ministered to for three years hearing some of the very ones he reached most to cheering the loudest for him to be crucified over Barabus, a known criminal. He knew very real physical pain when a cat o' nine tails whip slashed into the skin on His back and flesh on His cross.

Our High Priest is familiar with our lives from the inside. He knew having to tell His disciples a few days before that he would not be with them much longer. He knew just before his ministry officially started being tempted in the wilderness to throw himself off the side of a mountain.

Perhaps the most motivating thing to me though when I wonder if my Lord Jesus understands is knowing that He went to the cross. My little crosses in life have been nothing compared to the cross He had to bear. Whatever layers of pain I have endured, whatever tears I have cried, whatever physical aches and pains I have had, whatever relational stresses I may have, whatever happens around me I have never ever gone to a cross. I doubt you have gone to a cross as brutal as His either. If He has a greater level of experience than any of us have maybe it's about time that we consider that He also has a response to it that is worth our consideration.

What would happen if we asked his advice regarding our present afflictions? What Scriptures might He lead us to? What practical direction might he give us? What situations might He bring to our memories where we have overcome already but forgotten about?

When I have spoken with people who have attempted suicide I often hear stories of interventions and situations that can only be God. I can't tell you how many times when a person wanted to "end it all" a family member who wasn't supposed to come home at the time came home at a different time. I have also heard too many examples of people who planned and plotted ways to do the suicide "really good" so no one would find them for sure. One instance comes to mind where a young lady took a gun with her and planned and isolated place deep in the woods to go to. She got to the place where no one was in sight. She thought she was alone and was prepare to take her life "for good this time." But then- what do you know!!!- out of the blue as she looked at the gun and said a quick "I'm sorry" to God police showed up out of nowhere searching for another person and ended up discovering her. God wanted her to live. He has a plan for her life.

What would happen if we asked his advice regarding our present afflictions? What Scriptures might He lead us to? What practical direction might he give us? What situations might He bring to our memories where we have overcome already but forgotten about?

Perhaps you can recall a time in your life where a circumstance interrupted your plan. Maybe you can recall a situation that you thought was a random interruption that prevented your suicide. Did you ever consider that God is not done with you? God knows the plans and purposes for which he created you and maybe tried to show you how valuable you are in more ways than you possibly realize.

So many times people state to me, "I don't know why suicide attempts never work for me." Have you considered that God has His plans too beyond your own plans? He wants to intervene daily in our lives but often it is just not the way we desire. Our human desires are for the intervention to be something that stops the pain. But for God usually an intervention is not always about eliminating the stressful situation so you and I can learn to be calm in the storm.

It is not unlike when a storm was raging on the sea. The disciples, many of whom were fisherman and had faced storms before were freaked out because this storm was unlike any other. They had a sense of impending doom and fear. But Jesus' reaction was to speak to the storm with authority saying, "peace, peace. Be still." What if you and I would learn to perceive the waves in our lives correctly without magnifying them or becoming overly preoccupied and distracted by them?

Anxiety and depression lie to us. They get us living in the "as if" thinking. The problem is that they only tell us the negative "what ifs". They never tell the positive considerations. Let me urge you today that if you are going to waste your time thinking and preparing for a host of negative possibilities then you also might as well consider the equally likely possibility that something good can happen.

If you continue thinking negatively you will find the negative. If you ponder what the next negative possibility might be you can certainly find it. But if you ponder the next possibility that the voice of authority and peace in Jesus Christ can reign in your life as much as He did in the disciples' storm then just imagine the possibilities.

Let's practice. Instead of being ruled by the storm of chronic pain we'll choose to embrace the healing, health, and wholeness of a body "fearfully and wonderfully made" in Him that must line up with His purposes (see Psalm 139). Let's consider instead of getting another bad report that a helpful strategy and victory is coming your way for dealing with that situation. Let's consider that instead of running out of strengths and resources that God has resources and can speak to people in ways you have not even considered to help you.

We limit God so much. I can't say I understand all or even much of what He does and why He does it but I can certainly say that in many situations I can look back years after the fact to see a sense of perspective I did not have when I was in the middle of something.

The key is what we do with the preoccupation. Preoccupation with the unpleasant does not help. Instead, it cultivates more anxiety. Instead of living in the here and now enjoying possibilities that can turn around you live a helpless, hopeless, and paralyzed life. At the worst you stop caring for yourself, stops bathing, cleaning the house, or doing what is required day to day. It may get so bad that you no longer even go outside the house for groceries, a job, or to get mail.

I encourage you today to pray and consider God's positive Biblical alternatives to preoccupation with your pain. Philippians 4: 7-9 gives some good guidelines. It tells us the alternative qualities of healthier thoughts- they are good, holy, praiseworthy, of good report, and hope filled.

Use these qualities to measure your thoughts against. Do they line up with these or are they negative, preoccupied, degrading, death producing, and hopeless? Keep a notebook every time you are tempted to succumb to negativity. Fill in the blanks. In your frustrating situation what is....

    True?
    Honest?
    Just?
    Pure?
    Lovely?
    Of good report?

    Philippians advises us to think upon these qualities and attributes. My paraphrase is "be preoccupied with these." It is all about what you feed yourself. What you feed yourself will grow.

    Preoccupation with the negative possibilities can never bring peace. Yet the foolish way we tend to think is to believe that if I practice considering all the negatives I'll be ready for the worst." We also think, "If I do it (what is not working) a little more it will be better." But exactly the opposite happens. So our hearts end up open, exposed, vulnerable and shriveled with decay. What if we could just implement and practice Philippians chapter four until our hearts have a guard around them. A guarded heart is a protected heart. God wants to protect your heart. If need be He will even create within you "a new heart". (Psalm 51:10) Maybe your heart has been so burned by life that it does not know how to accept the good. He can create a heart capable of seeing beyond abuse, pain, sting, wrong to the light at the end of the tunnel.

A guarded heart is a protected heart. God wants to protect your heart. If need be He will even create within you "a new heart". (Psalm 51:10) Maybe your heart has been so burned by life that it does not know how to accept the good. He can create a heart capable of seeing beyond abuse, pain, sting, wrong to the light at the end of the tunnel.

I once preached a message called "If Today Could Be Your Resurrection Day." For most people this was a blessing. You may want renewed hope and resurrection but be afraid even of the newness because you cannot control it. You want things to happen on your terms. But what if you could undo fear of how the newness and freedom will happen? For God is a healer and deliverer and He comes for renewed hope.

It has become so easy and natural for people to become absorbed with their own lives. In fact one day while I was praying God showed me a vision of the nation of America with the word "entitlement" above it in big letters. All so often we are taught principles about "being your best self" that sound good but keep us in ruts. We are in a society which perpetuates the belief that you get what you put into life. There is certainly a lot of truth to this. God will not and cannot honor someone who does not follow His principles and honor Him. However, on the other hand, it is not solely what we put in that is all that matters.

For example, I can't even count how many time people have come to counseling with the misbelief that if they think they are a nice, ethical, moral or kind-hearted person that good things should happen to them. They believe that "good" people should have "good" things and "evil" people should have "bad" things happen to them. But this is not true. Life happens to everyone. The Bible tells us it "rains on the just and unjust" (Matthew 5:45)

Think of it this way. It is not because you have done all the good, right, strong, and perfect things that you should have a problem-free life. It is in spite of you and me that a merciful God would extend His grace to all who would freely accept it and abide by His principles.

Thinking about how much mercy, punishment or entitlement we or another deserves misses the point. At that point we become preoccupied with ourselves and the world around us rather than fixated on the underlying spiritual Biblical principles at work that we do not see.

Jesus made choices to respond to awful circumstances by doing several behaviors that today could also be of help to us. He got away and prayed. Several times in Scripture we hear that He "went to a remote place." (e.g. Mark 6:31, Matthew 14:13-14) After many of the accounts of miracles we hear him going away alone again to pray and be with the Father. He also focused as in the temptation in the wilderness account on what "was written." (Matthew 4:1-11) He knew that the Scriptures and holy writings were what is established in the heavens. He knew these are the more true and important account than the hunger and temptations He was feeling in the moment.

The problem is that we are so prone to self-pity. We love to tell stories about the troubles and trials we are going through. It can feel nice to get sympathy. It can be nice to get money, time, attention, or privileges from people. Have you ever realized though that there can be a thin line between sharing a need for prayer and turning it over to God and becoming preoccupied with the pressure? When we become preoccupied we have made the issue a God. I am not suggesting that we deny issues but rather than we admit issues with a balanced reaction to them.

We do not want to run the risk of idolatry to where we open ourselves up to a broken records of "woe is me. My life is so awful. There is no way out of this mess." Those are the unending cries of someone who eventually may become suicidal. They have idolized their pain and struggles rather than rightly exalting the ability of the King of

Kings and Lord of Lords in the midst of things. Maybe you never thought of it this way.

I had not thought of it as idolatry until I really studied more about what happens when people wallow in self-pity. Proverbs tells us, "as a man thinks so is he." (Proverbs 23:7) Imagine someone thinking and pondering over and over how awful things are, how there is no hope how life is over. He or she will start living as if life is over. And eventually he or she will act out through suicide his or her life really being over.

It is up to us to decide what we will focus on. There is a Scripture that asks, "whose report will you believe?" (Isaiah 53:1) There is an option. You can choose to believe the reports which have brought nothing good to you so far. Dwelling on those negative reports has kept you hopeless, helpless, and stuck. Your other option is to believe the alternative report that "God will turn things around for the good of those who love him and are called according to His purpose." (Romans 8:28)

I encourage you to make up some worksheets in a journal to help you when stresses come. List each key word or phrase in Philippians 4. What is true? What is holy? What is the good report in the seemingly bad report of others or of the way circumstances feel? Read these alternative Bible based truths over and over till you begin to believe them. Reflect on them. Ask God to make these truths real to you. Find and search Scriptures which support the alternative Biblical truths. If you are not versed in how to do Bible studies, see if you can get a copy of the "Bible Promise Book" which itemizes Scriptures by alphabetical topic. So if you are anxious you can read about Bible verses for fighting anxiety or if you are discouraged and helpless you can read about God's help and hope.

"The problem is that we are so prone to self-pity. We love to tell stories about the troubles and trials we are going through. It can feel nice to get sympathy. It can be nice to get money, time, attention, or privileges from people. Have you ever realized though that there can be a thin line between sharing a need for prayer and turning it over to God and becoming preoccupied with the pressure? When we become preoccupied we have made the issue a God. I am not suggesting that we deny issues but rather than we admit issues with a balanced reaction to them.

Since it can be natural to be self-preoccupied it may be a real stretch of the imagination to dream of doing otherwise especially when stresses abound. There are some Scriptures that help us learn about how to make that shift to being preoccupied with Jesus Christ, what is Biblically and spiritually true, and what brings life and hope. For example, we can remind ourselves of what Hebrews 12:1 states:

> Wherefore seeing we also are compassed about with so great a cloud of witnesses, let us lay aside every weight, and the sin which doth so easily beset us, and let us run with patience the race that is set before us, looking unto Jesus the author and finisher of our faith; who for the joy that was set before him endured the cross, despising the shame, and is set down at the right hand of the throne of God.

We can set our minds on things that are above, not on things that are on earth. (Colossians 3:2) We do this by being more preoccupied with seeking the kingdom of God and His righteousness. (Matthew 6:33) We do this by "forgetting what lies behind and straining forward to what lies ahead, pressing on toward the goal for the prize of the upward call of God in Christ Jesus." (Philippians 3:12-14)

Another way to kill the idol of self-preoccupation is by focusing on the needs of others. Acts 20:35 tells us that "it is more blessed to give than receive." Have you ever noticed that when you are focused on helping others, praying, and when you take care of others that God takes care of you? When you love others- the very mark being a disciple of Christ- you become free from self-absorption. (John 13:14) What would life be like if we followed the command to "do nothing from selfish ambition or conceit, but in humility count others more significant than yourselves. Let each of you look not only to his own interests, but also to the interests of others. (Philippians 2:3–4)

Your understanding will lead you astray. It will keep you bound. It will make you want to give up more than you ever felt like giving up- even to the point of killing yourself. There is an alternative in Proverbs 3:5-6: "Trust in the Lord with all your heart, and do not lean on your own understanding. In all your ways acknowledge him, and he will make straight your paths." Making straight does not mean you will never have troubles. It just means that He will keep you centered in your walk. He knows there will be flood waters and fiery trials. That is why He says in Isaiah 43:2:

when you pass through the waters, I will be with you; and through the rivers, they shall not overwhelm you; when you walk through fire you shall not be burned, and the flame shall not consume you.

God sees ability in us enables us to live differently than the paralysis we have resolved ourselves to. That is why He treats us like the man waiting by the pool at Bethesda for nearly forty years. He comes to where you are and with a voice of authority says loud and clear, "take up your mat and walk." (John 5:8) He doesn't talk with you for hours about the forty years of all you've tried that hasn't worked. He doesn't get into what kept you on the sidelines lounging on your mat complaining and waiting while others got the help and healing you did not get. He just tells you to walk. In other words, live like you are healthy. Live like you are not depressed. Live like a happy, healthy person.

How is this possible you may think? I like to describe it as working the process in reverse. When we hit a wall we can no longer wait for a feeling of being motivated, happy, encouraged and jubilant you will at to come over us to get us going. We have to reflect on the times- even years ago- when we were happier, healthier, and more whole people. What were we doing then? What faith were we drawing on then? What resources were we implementing? What behaviors were we doing? Then do what you don't feel like doing. Do it whether you feel it or not. The more you do the behaviors that were opposite depression and anxiety, helplessness, and despair the more natural those behaviors will become. It is just like muscles in your body. If you do not exercise the things which Biblically lead to abundant life and wholeness then you will spiritually atrophy.

Then do not do those live giving things just once or twice and expect a huge change. Allow the Holy Spirit to sacrificially do them through you repetitively. Job 17:9 tells us that "the righteous keep moving forward, and those with clean hands become stronger and stronger." The phrase "keep moving" suggests that they don't do it once or twice only. Instead, we hear another reference to the lifestyle of walking in the Spirit which is a lifestyle of letting the power of God overtake you and do through you what you cannot do yourself.

I like the way the psalmist puts it: "My health may fail, and my spirit may grow weak, but God remains the strength of my heart; he is mine forever" (Psalms 73:26). Notice the emphasis on the word "my." My anything will fail. When will we get that in our silly, foolish heads? My everything will always fall short. But His strength is perfected in my weakness. (2 Corinthians 12:9)

There is another special key in the aforementioned verse in Psalms 73:6. Notice the word "BUT." We forget to tell ourselves the whole truth. Often we tell ourselves the first part about the feelings of being a failure and weak but we do not continue to talk about the faithfulness of God in spite of us. We must cultivate the memory of the benefits of relationship with God. (Psalm 103:2)

2 Corinthians 5:1-21 agrees that:

> while we are still in this tent, we groan, being burdened—not that we would be unclothed, but that we would be further clothed, so that what is mortal may be swallowed up by life. He who has prepared us for this very thing is God, who has given us the Spirit as a guarantee.

So all the pain you have been through- all the layers of the onion peel we spoke about earlier are for this very reason- that His abundant resurrection life may swallow up your mortal, feeble efforts. Will you let His mantle of healing, newness and victory cover your efforts? Will you let Him be the Author and Finisher of your faith? (Hebrews 12:2).

So all the pain you have been through- all the layers of the onion peel we spoke about earlier are for this very reason- that His abundant resurrection life may swallow up your mortal, feeble efforts. Will you let His mantle of healing, newness and victory cover your efforts?

There is surely a distinction between our ways and God's ways as the Bible confirms in Isaiah 55:8-9 when it states:

> For my thoughts are not your thoughts, neither are your ways my ways, says the LORD. For as the heavens are higher than the earth, so are my ways higher than your ways, and my thoughts than your thoughts.

Can you accept the fact that His ways are better? Will you humble yourself knowing that the God of this universe knows a thing or two more than you and I know? It is not too late.

Control is an illusion. We deceive ourselves if we think we can control and master anything. Where have our attempts to control gotten us? Might it be better if we lay it all down and try not controlling anything but receiving what He decides and equips us for in His perfect strength and ability and timing?

Today can be a new start. We can leave former things behind. We can walk as new creations allowing the power of the living God to overtake our perspectives and attitudes on life issues. We can "let our eyes gaze directly forward and let our gaze be straight." (Proverbs 4:25) It is possible to have a good ending to the story of your life that at present feels awful. Remember there is never a testimony of God's goodness without the test. We can speak like Paul in Acts 20:24:

> But none of these things move me, neither count I my life dear unto myself, so that I might finish my course with joy, and the ministry, which I have

received of the Lord Jesus, to testify the gospel of the grace of God.

In conclusion, we can choose what we are preoccupied about. While no one can promise no distress or trouble in life we can find rest in the midst of it all. When in distress we cry out to the Lord and pray to God for help He "hears from his sanctuary; our cries to him reach His ears." (Psalm 18:6) Become preoccupied with the God who delights in hearing your cry.

Lessons From The Bible About Healing

There are several examples of people healed throughout Scripture. Let's look at a handful of them to see how eager, ready and available the Lord Jesus Christ is to be a present healer for you in your darkest hour. In Mark 5: 3-20 we see the story of a possessed man who lived in tombs. Let's read about it:

> And they came over unto the other side of the sea, into the country of the Gadarenes. And when he was come out of the ship, immediately there met him out of the tombs a man with an unclean spirit, who had his dwelling among the tombs; and no man could bind him, no, not with chains: Because that he had been often bound with fetters and chains, and the chains had been plucked asunder by him, and the fetters broken in pieces: neither could any man tame him. And always, night and day, he was in the mountains, and in the tombs, crying, and cutting himself with stones. But when he saw Jesus afar off, he ran and worshipped him,

And cried with a loud voice, and said, What have I to do with thee, Jesus, thou Son of the most high God? I adjure thee by God, that thou torment me not. For he said unto him, Come out of the man, thou unclean spirit. And he asked him, What is thy name? And he answered, saying, My name is Legion: for we are many. And he besought him much that he would not send them away out of the country. Now there was there nigh unto the mountains a great herd of swine feeding. And all the devils besought him, saying, Send us into the swine, that we may enter into them. Jesus gave them leave. And the unclean spirits went out, and entered into the swine: and the herd ran violently down a steep place into the sea, (they were about two thousand;) and were choked in the sea.

And they that fed the swine fled, and told it in the city, and in the country. And they went out to see what it was that was done. And they come to Jesus, and see him that was possessed with the devil, and had the legion, sitting, and clothed, and in his right mind: and they were afraid. And they that saw it told them how it befell to him that was possessed with the devil, and also concerning the swine. And they began to pray him to depart out of their coasts. And when he was come into the ship, he that had been possessed with the devil prayed him that he might be with him. Howbeit Jesus suffered him not, but saith unto him, Go home to thy friends, and tell them how great things the Lord hath done for thee, and hath had compassion on thee. And he departed, and began to publish in Decapolis how great things Jesus had done for him: and all men did marvel.

Originally chains could not subdue this man's agitation. Not only his town but even the whole region of the Gerasenes knew of him and wanted nothing to do with him. That is where our first lesson comes in. Often Jesus has a heart that people do not have. When people don't want anything to do with our hurts, pains, and issues Jesus says, "bring it on! I am here for you."

If this happened today most ministers would probably say, "why in the world would I want to pray for a man who lives in tombs and cuts himself?" They would fear the man and his strength. They would fear the agitation might turn on them. They would maybe not want to even be seen praying for someone who lives in tombs and is different or unusual. But the fact is Jesus passed by this region and this specific man. Secondly, we see the depth of the weight of his pain. He was in so much pain that he was a self mutilator. He would take jagged stones and use the rough edges to cut himself. Imagine approaching one in pain who doesn't look so pretty and has scars on his or her arms or legs from cutting. He did not just have one simple easy issue that could quickly be talked out. No. This man had many deep issues that bound him. That's why the demons in him stated the name is "Legion" or a group.

If you are reading this book I imagine that you may feel at times like there are layers of stuff that have piled up and you've wondered if anyone cares. But if you look at this example you can see clearly that Jesus cared. He passed by. He didn't circle and walk around the town. He went right to the tombs. Imagine the Savior of the world going into the tombs to offer new life to a man who was living in pain as if he was already emotionally dead.

Not only was he cutting but imagine the rejection from a whole town and region hating you. He knew no social supports. He knew not one "hello" or kind word or prayer. He was shunned and forgotten but not by Jesus. Maybe you have felt like with your issues you are shunned, forgotten rejected and forsaken. Maybe you have burned every bridge with your family, friends, and others. There is one support system who will be "a friend that sticks closer than a brother." (Proverbs 18:24) His name is Jesus. And He will make a point of coming to the place you are in just to reach out to you if you will allow him.

The key is not to get in the rut and assume that God must be exactly like the people who rejected you. Sometimes we make that mistake. But thankfully God is exactly the opposite. He became flesh to us to extend His support with full healing and wholeness to us in a very real and practical way.

Let's see another example in Luke 4:31-37:

> And came down to Capernaum, a city of Galilee, and taught them on the sabbath days. And they were astonished at his doctrine: for his word was with power. And in the synagogue there was a man, which had a spirit of an unclean devil, and cried out with a loud voice, saying, Let us alone; what have we to do with thee, thou Jesus of Nazareth? Art thou come to destroy us? I know thee who thou art; the Holy One of God. And Jesus rebuked him, saying, Hold thy peace, and come out of him. And when the devil had thrown him in the midst, he came out of him, and hurt him not. And they were all amazed, and spake among themselves, saying, What a word is this! for with authority and power he commandeth

the unclean spirits, and they come out. And the fame of him went out into every place of the country round about.

Again Jesus approached the one who was bound. Even the congregation was not helping him. Sometimes we can be in the middle of a group and just be one hidden, nameless face. We hide the hurt and pain. Unless we make known what is going on by going to an altar for prayer or calling one of the minsters for personal ministry we may get nowhere. But to Jesus we are not just one nameless face in creation. We are all unique, special and worth helping.

Matthew 8:2-3 also gives an example of an incurable contagious disease of leprosy. Leprosy was open wounds and sores. If a person was a leper by law the townspeople were to cry "leper" if he was even coming at a distance. Imagine the pain and rejection. Maybe you do not have big sores on your skin but maybe you have felt like when people see you coming they go the opposite direction like you have something negative to spread to them. Maybe you have been waiting all your life for someone to touch your sores- be they physical scabs or heart scars. Let's receive hope as we hear this Bible account:

And, behold, there came a leper and worshipped him, saying, Lord, if thou wilt, thou canst make me clean. And Jesus put forth his hand, and touched him, saying, I will; be thou clean. And immediately his leprosy was cleansed.

The thing that is so important here is that this man with leprosy stated, "Lord if you are willing." Is that your heart's cry? Do you believe the Lord is willing or does part of you say, "I want the healing but maybe the Lord will not help me like other people have." Maybe you've grown accustomed to being alone because the pain of dealing with people in real life is just too much. You don't have to watch them run. You can start accepting you as the non-contagious healed one today.

In another account in Matthew 8:10-13 Jesus did much because he saw great faith of a soldier.

> When Jesus heard it, he marvelled, and said to them that followed, Verily I say unto you, I have not found so great faith, no, not in Israel. And I say unto you, That many shall come from the east and west, and shall sit down with Abraham, and Isaac, and Jacob, in the kingdom of heaven. But the children of the kingdom shall be cast out into outer darkness: there shall be weeping and gnashing of teeth. And Jesus said unto the centurion, Go thy way; and as thou hast believed, so be it done unto thee. And his servant was healed in the selfsame hour.

We can learn from this account that Jesus stated to the soldier that the healing was related to what he believed. This goes back to the principles we talked about earlier regarding paying attention to our beliefs, actions, and speech. What do you really believe today? Do you believe that enough is enough and that it is time for the dark hour and seasons of your life to end? Do you believe that when you invite Jesus into your situation right now as you read this book that what has been a struggle and problem for years can be healed?

Note also that the account above says that the servant was healed in that moment. What is cool is that the servant himself may not have even had faith. Sometimes we are believing for a spouse, family members, or another than needs healing. Can you stretch your faith today for them? Remember that even a little tiny faith the size of a mustard seed can move mountains. (Luke 17:6) When you take your little belief and put it in Jesus' victorious nail scarred hands expect something amazing to happen.

We can also read another account of healing in Matthew 15:22-28:

> And, behold, a woman of Canaan came out of the same coasts, and cried unto him, saying, Have mercy on me, O Lord, thou son of David; my daughter is grievously vexed with a devil. But he answered her not a word. And his disciples came and besought him, saying, Send her away; for she crieth after us. But he answered and said, I am not sent but unto the lost sheep of the house of Israel. Then came she and worshipped him, saying, Lord, help me. But he answered and said, It is not meet to take the children's bread, and to cast it to dogs. And she said, Truth, Lord: yet the dogs eat of the crumbs which fall from their masters' table. Then Jesus answered and said unto her, O woman, great is thy faith: be it unto thee even as thou wilt. And her daughter was made whole from that very hour.

Recall earlier that we spoke about the importance of what we are doing, saying, and thinking in the pain. This woman came worshipping. What a challenge that would be for so many of us. Can you imagine coming before God kneeling and worshipping, praising, and living as if the miracle help you needed already happened? That sounds impossible but with God's grace that's exactly what the woman did. And the neat thing is that the account says she was "cured at that moment." As soon as we admit fully our weakness, sin, or inability and cry to God for help while revering the majesty of who He is something great can happen. Dark midnight hours become bright morning dawns when you and I have positive expectation and gratitude.

Lest you think that whatever your dark hour is or your situation that they are not covered by this healing let me offer you another Scripture passage from Matthew 15:29- 31:

And Jesus departed from thence, and came nigh unto the sea of Galilee; and went up into a mountain, and sat down there. And great multitudes came unto him, having with them those that were lame, blind, dumb, maimed, and many others, and cast them down at Jesus' feet; and he healed them: Insomuch that the multitude wondered, when they saw the dumb to speak, the maimed to be whole, the lame to walk, and the blind to see: and they glorified the God of Israel.

What I like about this passage is that it includes all sorts of people: lame, maimed, blind, dumb, and many others. You may be part of these so this promise is for you. Your midnight hour is meaningful to Jesus Christ. In case you doubt that these Scriptures cover you or that your specific issues, let me offer you Mathew 12:15: "being aware of this Jesus went away from there. And many people, joined and accompanied Him and He cured all of them." This is the type of Scripture I really like because it says "all." I believe that whatever your midnight hour situation it is covered in that "all."

If you feel you are too weak to ask for help and too doubtful let's confess that unbelief and even now ask God for help to believe life can be different. This pain and trauma, this depression, anxiety, physical issues, and emotional cares are getting you nowhere. Matthew 18: 18-20 states:

> Verily I say unto you, Whatsoever ye shall bind on earth shall be bound in heaven: and whatsoever ye shall loose on earth shall be loosed in heaven. Again I say unto you, That if two of you shall agree on earth as touching anything that they shall ask, it shall be done for them of my Father which is in heaven. For where two or three are gathered together in my name, there am I in the midst of them.

I pray now in agreement with the words and examples of the Bible and with the faith God is able to give you now that He will begin that complete and perfect work in your life toward total healing and wholeness. You may not fathom how but all things are possible to them that believe.(Matthew 19:26) We can believe together now. He cares for you.

If Jesus had to pass by a tomb, go to a place where people were rejected, be seen around the unseemingly, and talk to those others gave up on a longtime ago He certainly is ready to meet with you. Why can't that meeting start now? Cry, ask, make known your need, and kneel and adore him even in your situation as the woman above did earlier.

God works in different ways with different people. But once you reach out to Him your life cannot be the same. Let's rejoice even now that what has felt like the deepest, darkest of nights is soon going to be a memory. Let's think about how God has to be faithful to his consistent character of caring about His creation intimately. Allow him to come to you and personally visit with you in your situation. Allow Him to be your support system and your king, help, redeemer, and life giver.

*As soon as we admit fully our
weakness, sin, or inability
and cry to God for help while
revering the majesty of who
He is something great can
happen. Dark midnight hours
become bright morning dawns
when you and I have positive
expectation and gratitude.*

The Beautiful Places of The Ashes

One of the most meaningful and important messages I preached was called "The Beautiful Places of The Ashes." I would like to share with you some of the most important concepts and principles I taught which are all outlined in Scripture. As strange as the title sounds, my hope is that we all come to realize that usually in life that what we do in the place of the hurt, pain, death, loss, and unexpected trials determines what comes next spiritually.

The ashes were symbolic in the Old Testament of the sacrifice for atonement of sin or the burnt offerings that were given in the temple by the priest (see Leviticus 6:9-11). The ashes burned all night. Thankfully today you and I do not have to go through rituals and burning of sacrifices to atone for sin but Jesus Christ has been made our sacrifice. We can approach Him with all our hurts, pains, and problems. In doing so the place of what we see as ashes can become the most beautiful place we have ever been.

Sounds crazy, right? It does not makes sense until we realize what the ashes are all about. First, there is a realization that our efforts are at best futile. We keep doing things which make us still unclean and imperfect before God. We keep trying to do more of the same things which keep us in ruts and sins which displease God and keep our pain going. All the while we are promised in the Bible that He gives us "beauty for ashes and gladness for mourning" (Isaiah 61:1-11) How wonderful does that sound! I bet right about now you could use beauty if you're feeling a little bit worn by life. I bet right now you could use a bit of joy to be strengthened where your hurt, pain, tears, and despair have left you mourning relentlessly.

One day when I was praying for someone in a counseling session God spoke to me to tell her something. I have never forgotten this is my own life and continued to encourage others with what God spoke. He said, "celebrate what you do not see. Then you will see what you can celebrate." Did you get that? We are to think about what we can have gratitude for already so we will be better able to perceive and receive when things turn around.

Let's take time to do that even now. Reflect on the things in your life where by now you would have been a worse mess, been troubled more, been dead, been immobilized by fear and sadness had God not been there. We are told in the Bible to "forget not His benefits." (Psalm 103:2) This is critical because when we forget what God has already done and how He has been faithful so far we tend to believe a lie that nothing is going on for us in the meantime. I encourage you to write a thanksgiving or gratitude journal. During one of the hardest years of my life I did that. I forced myself daily to find the good, to celebrate the joy, to thank God for things like seeing another day and strength to endure. I learned to appreciate the seemingly "small" things each day. I discovered that there were a multitude of reasons to be grateful in the ashes. I did not necessarily have to wait for my situation to change to be thankful but I could practice praising God in the place where it felt like all my hopes and dreams had ended. In the long run I ended up with a full notebook of personal reasons to thank God. To this day, twenty years later I still open that notebook when I am discouraged and read how many blessings I learned about when I was actively grateful during that rough year. The more grateful I was in the process the more things began to unfold that had not been expected by the end of that year.

What could possibly be good about our pains and suffering? Ashes are a symbol of purification. Something changes within us when we go through rough times. Did you ever notice that it is extremely rare for great change to occur when life is seemingly going well? In order for us to experience a resurrection and newness where our hope that seems gone is revived by God Himself we must let our way of looking at and doing things die.

There are some key transformations that happen at the place of the ashes if you and I will allow them. You likely do not know all the details of what is going on. You may feel like God is silent or that the next steps in life are unknown. Usually it is exactly the opposite. That is when we are expected to stand in what we know and hold to Scripture while God is working behind the scenes. God is always doing something but we may not see it that way in our limited mindsets. We may think nothing is going on but God may actually be making a whole new and improved way for you if you will allow His grace to carry you through the waiting time.

You may go through a time of searching and seeking for meaning through prayer, Bible reading, worship, and thinking or talking stresses through. After having done this searching you will better be able to line up with the Word of God. Doing Godly things are not always easy and natural especially when people feel in a bind. When we are in tough situations and squeezed what we are really made of comes out. God can make and mold us to be resilient and strong enough to operate in the victorious power and authority He has already given us in Jesus Christ.

Hebrews 3 says something interesting. It says that "by faith the ashes still speak." This means that when people reflect on your life it is often how you responded when you were in a jam and the character you demonstrated that they commemorate. Recall eulogies of people. People never say, "so and so is a real pain in the neck. He couldn't handle stress well." No. They say things like, "she was an excellent mother who gave her all even when she lacked things herself" or "he was a caring, giving person who made time for others even when he suffered from his own health problems." It is interesting that after someone dies we tend to really find out what people think of them. Why not allow the times of life's trials and ashes to help them speak well about us and, more importantly, about our God while we are still alive?

There is never a testimony without a test. If things we so good and easy all the time then there would be no real need to rejoice when then blessing comes. It is because there have been tough things to endure that we have a testimony. The point is we also do not have to wait to share a testimony until we are on the other side of our problem. Remember when Jesus told the disciples they were "going to the other side" (Mark 4:35) He said this while huge waves and storms were hitting the boat they were in buffeting it back and forth. Likewise, He tells us, "you are going to the other side of this problem by My strength and grace." He doesn't tell us this when the sea is calm but when the waves of life look like tsunamis you will drown in. Write down now the victory you are believing

God for and live as I the waves are not your reality but going to the other side is.

The ashes are your place of decision. What will you do with Christ? Will you have tunnel vision on the problems and continue to be stuck? Will you sink in the mire as Scripture calls it? Or will you allow yourself to see the fresh water of the Lord and His resurrection washing away the filth and dirt while you are in the process of coming through something uncomfortable? Will you sit in the ashes of life stresses calm and waiting on God knowing that the resurrection and life is sitting there with you. Thus, dark becomes light and mourning and pain turns to rejoicing.

The key is the language we tell our minds and speak to others. If we talk in terms of "someday life will be better" or "if only _____ happens then I could be happy" we will be stuck and helpless. But if we admit the feelings yet more importantly admit that we are in process of going to the other side then we will have a hope no one and nothing can take away.

This may not be the easiest thing to do on your won. That is why I would highly recommend having someone who can help you be accountable during the times where all you see are the ashes. When we see aches, pain, hurt, and tears it can be easy to make impulsive, unhealthy decisions on our own. However, if we have even one believer, a prayer line with someone who prays the Bible, or a church ministry who will lift us up we can make it through.

This is where the Holy Spirit, God's real presence in the moment of the ashes is needed. As you read John 14:15-17 hear it as if Jesus is speaking it directly to you since it is just as applicable to you as anyone else today:

157

> If ye love me, keep my commandments. And I will pray the Father, and He shall give you another Comforter, that He may abide with you forever; even the Spirit of truth; whom the world cannot receive, because it sees him not, neither knows him: but you know him; for he dwells with you, and shall be in you.

The Holy Spirit according to John 14:26 also teaches you and brings to your remembrance all the valuable lessons that Jesus has conveyed in your life thus far. When we don't know what to pray Romans 8:26 says that the Holy Spirit assists us. As a result we can experience freedom. Pain that's yielded to God gives way to new perspective and hope we could not see before. Therefore, my prayer for you is the same Paul prayed for the church in Romans 15:13:

> Now the God of hope fill you with all joy and peace in believing, that ye may abound in hope, through the power of the Holy Ghost.

The only way we can discover hope is by what we do in the place of the ashes.

Who Will You Serve?

W hat if today could be your resurrection day? It is all your choice. The circumstances don't have to determine the outcome as we have seen. Instead, your reaction coupled with God's ability and authority can be a mighty force to be reckoned with.

There are several key principles we have learned so far which are essential to victory over this present dark seeming hour:

- The temptation is always to look at what happens in the natural as determining things rather than what is unseen supernaturally
- It is not about what happens as much as about our perspective of what happened.
- We must allow our perspective to be covered over by God (regardless of what people have done to us)
- It is possible to get rid of the graveclothes of victimology, blame, bitterness, anger, depression, paralysis, habits or sins in reactions to what someone else did

The key question: do you really want a resurrection (or do you just say it?)

Let's refer to Ephesians 4:17-32.

This I say therefore, and testify in the Lord, that ye henceforth walk not as other Gentiles walk, in the vanity of their mind, having the understanding darkened, being alienated from the life of God through the ignorance that is in them, because of the blindness of their heart: who being past feeling have given themselves over unto lasciviousness, to work all uncleanness with greediness. But ye have not so learned Christ; If so be that ye have heard him, and have been taught by him, as the truth is in Jesus: That ye put off concerning the former conversation the old man, which is corrupt according to the deceitful lusts; And be renewed in the spirit of your mind; And that ye put on the new man, which after God is created in righteousness and true holiness. Wherefore putting away lying, speak every man truth with his neighbor: for we are members one of another. Be ye angry, and sin not: let not the sun go down upon your wrath. Neither give place to the devil. Let him that stole steal no more: but rather let him labor, working with his hands the thing which is good, that he may have to give to him that needs. Let no corrupt communication proceed out of your mouth, but that which is good to the use of edifying, that it may minister grace unto the hearers. And grieve not the Holy Spirit of God, whereby ye are sealed unto the day of redemption. Let all bitterness, and wrath, and anger, and clamor, and evil speaking, be put away from you, with all malice: And be ye kind one to another, tenderhearted, forgiving one another, even as God for Christ's sake hath forgiven you.

The Secret Is In Your "Eshcol"

You may have never heard of a place called Eshcol. I think, however, the lessons about Eshcol can be useful in helping us put the darkest hour in perspective. Let's start by reading about Eshcol from Numbers 13:23-26:

And they came unto the brook of Eshcol, and cut down from thence a branch with one cluster of grapes, and they bare it between two upon a staff; and they brought of the pomegranates, and of the figs. The place was called the brook Eshcol, because of the cluster of grapes which the children of Israel cut down from thence. And they returned from searching of the land after forty days. And they went and came to Moses, and to Aaron, and to all the congregation of the children of Israel, unto the wilderness of Paran, to Kadesh; and brought back word unto them, and unto all the congregation, and shewed them the fruit of the land.

We all are aware of the feeling of being in utter dryness and wilderness spiritually, when all one wants is something to saturate one's thirst. But understand that the Israelites were not only in a natural wilderness, but they were also in a spiritual wilderness. When they got to Eshcol it was a valley. It was a place where they saw their foes and focused on the seeming largeness of the opposition. It was a place where all but two grown Israelite men sent to spy out the land came back complaining that they considered themselves small as grasshoppers (see

Numbers 13: 32-33). In the valley they were focused on expecting to be devoured. This problem is the same as the problem you and I face today. Rather than seeing the valley as just another place for God to show up they saw the valley as a different, new obstacle which seemed impossible in the natural to overcome. Sounds a lot like the perspectives we struggle with in our darkest hour today.

A few people were able to be quieted physically and spiritually even in this dry wilderness. Able to look beyond the apparent dryness they discovered that the very place of the valley was the place of great fruit. There were even clusters in the valley- not just isolated bits and pieces of fruit but whole groupings of fruit. The fruit was not in some nice remote peaceful village where there were no giants or no opposition. No- the fruit was in the land where the seeming giants and worst opposition was.

Herein lies the choice. Eschol always represents the place of decision. The Israelites had to choose to either focus on the seeming giants- the largeness of the opposition in the land-or to focus on the clusters of fruit. Similarly, we are told throughout Scripture that today in our own lives we will not be without trouble but we can choose to focus on the seeming trouble or the clusters of the anointing.

We must choose in our own Eshcols whether we will go forward or backward, whether we will cower in the face of what our own understanding and perception tells us or whether we will press on believing that what God says is absolutely true. We must make a decision. To stand in the crossroads and do nothing is not an option. Either we ultimately decide to back off in fear or we choose to move on in the faith which the Lord Himself provides for the journey. It boils down to what we do with Scripture and experience of God's personhood.

*We must choose in our own
Eshcols whether we will
go forward or backward,
whether we will cower in
the face of what our own
understanding and perception
tells us or whether we will
press on believing that what
God says is absolutely true.
We must make a decision. To
stand in the crossroads and
do nothing is not an option.
Either we ultimately decide to
back off in fear or we choose to
move on in the faith which the
Lord Himself provides
for the journey.*

It is all a matter of perspective. For example, some hear the Scripture "no weapon formed against me shall prosper"(Isaiah 54:17) and they get upset thinking "great, that means that weapons will be formed." Others look at the same Scripture and are excited for the victory because whether or not weapons are formed "greater is he within me than he that is in the world." (1 John 4:4) Some read about the armor of God in Ephesians, particularly the part that says "that you may be able to quench the fiery darts" (Ephesians 6:16) with terror at the thoughts of the darts coming at them. Others recall that the same power that was in Christ Jesus through the precious Holy Spirit is today the very exact same anointing within them. If you and I are to be victorious overcomers we must focus on the knowledge that "even greater things than [that which Jesus Christ did] shall they do" (John 14:12) through that same power of the Holy Spirit.

Hear brother and sister with ears of the Spirit even now for the cluster here that was put on that pole even in Numbers is the very same cluster (the fullness of the anointing of the Holy Spirit) in the New Testament that was put on the tree at Calvary. The cluster resided within Jesus Christ in much the same way that the cluster (the fullness) of the Holy Spirit resides within us as consecrated believers today.

The problem is that we tend to look at the tree. We become so distracted by our crosses and "calvaries." We become hyperfocused on the pain of the dying to self, the waiting, and enduring because we have forgotten that it is not our works that can help any of us to overcome Calvary.

Recall Jesus' test and temptation before his official ministry began. The test was one of Satan coming to Him and trying to get him to respond in His own strength- whether it be turning stones into bread for physical satisfaction of his hunger or throwing himself down off a mountain to gain the kingdoms of the world (see Matthew chapter 4). The venue may be different in our lives but the tactic remains the same. The sly, cunning voice of that same serpent in the garden of Eden or at Jesus' temptation in the wilderness is the same sly voice trying to speak the lie "do it on your own" as if we have ever had any resources that we can accomplish anything. May we not "think more highly of ourselves than we should" (Romans 12:3) but may be have sober judgment (1 Titus 3:2,11; Timothy 2:2-6, 1 Peter 1:13, 4:7, 5:8) of our natural inabilities and the supernatural abilities of the precious Holy Spirit.

Another problem we tend to have is that we tend to think that somehow although Jesus Christ through the Holy Spirit's power is the only own who overcame and victoriously ever arose and defeated sin and death that somehow that strength is lessened today. We think partially because we have been mistaught in our churches that it is absolutely not possible that the anointing and breakthrough could be in the valley. That just seems contrary to our reason. But what if the God whose "thoughts are not our thoughts" and whose "ways are not our ways" (Isaiah 55:8) specifically chose or allowed that valley in your life to be the very vehicle through which to manifest the cluster of the fruit of the Spirit? What if just as with Christ Jesus Himself your greatest victory in life is in the valley- at your Golgotha, your Calvary, your "place of the skull" literally where you least own your life?

Throughout Scripture we see the principle that blessing is linked to the degree to which we are willing to fellowship with Christ in the fullness of all of who He is, including the suffering, shaping, and molding of our precious Potter as He deems is necessary for our character development in Him. Song of Solomon 1:13-14 states that "my beloved [shepherd] is to me like a [scent] bag of myrrh that lies in my bosom. My beloved shepherd is to me a cluster of henna flowers in the vineyards of En-gedi [famed for its fragrant shrubs]."

En-gedi is a place of many rough rocks and crevices that are seemingly impossible to pass. It is a place which looks to be difficult to endure. En-gedi is where many goats hid in crevices of rocks as they climbed up places that were virtually impenetrable by others.

It also is a place of decision. We could look at the places in our lives whereby we see what seems to us to be impenetrable or we could look in faith at the crevices in the rock (our Rock, Jesus Christ) in whom we hide. King David was often found among the rocks of En-gedi. En-gedi was where Saul would seek for King David.

We have this idea that the cattle graze on nice even plots of well-kept manicured lawns. But the reality is that the sheep and goats actually grazed in the rocky cliffs and mountains whereby their trust every step of the way had to be in their shepherd. This remains an essential principle for us today if we want to be among the cluster of the choice, anointed grapes. We still must walk along those places we may not desire to go but where our trust is in our Great Shepherd who guides us over cliffs , crevices, and jagged edges to graze on revelations which can only be found there.

We tend to look at the roughness of the terrain. Christian maturity, however, looks at the experience of the guide. Do we actually think that our limited mindsets can outshine the perfect experience of the almighty God? Do we actually think we know more about the terrain based on our own understanding?

There is another interesting aside here. In the midst of the rough terrain is the life. En-gedi was not only known for rough, rocky terrain but was also known for year round life-giving springs of water. All sorts of plant and animals thrive in that atmosphere. The water is also bottled to drink.

We see Scriptural principles in action. The Great Shepherd is Jesus Christ Himself (see Psalm 23). Yet in being clustered in and abiding with our Great Shepherd there is "a [scent] bag of myrrh." (v.13) Myrrh is one of the three gifts given to Jesus at birth which represents both for Him and for us the element of suffering through the valleys of life. It is used in embalming. On the other hand it is called by many "the balm of Gilead" and is looked upon highly for its medicinal and healing properties. Though representative of suffering its weight value has remained nearly equal to gold.

Hear this spiritually- though representative of suffering the value of the price of the journey one takes is worth (literally) its weight in gold. In Scripture we are told that the journey, the shaping and molding, the abiding with Christ all has to do with the ultimate outcome of being "whole, complete , and lacking nothing in Him (James 1:4)."

Notice that the blossoming cluster of henna was in En-gedi. You may be tempted to think that because Scripture states that En-gedi is a vineyard that again we are talking of a lush fruit-filled land much like the wine country of southern California here in the United States. However, this could not be farther from the truth. En-gedi was an area of wilderness located in the Dead Sea region.

Wilderness and valleys (whether they be Eschol or En-gedi or Calvary) are absolutely essential for the making of the cluster of anointing. They are essential for effective transition from the darkest hour to the brightest dawn.

We would all like to think that somehow we could learn every spiritual lesson and achieve every blessing even through the pleasant times of life. Yet the fact remains that it is only in the places of pressing that one's true character is shaped and revealed. It is often primarily in those places we cry out to the Lord to be who He is and can only be. It is often in those places that we are sober enough to realize who we are not.

In the example from Song of Solomon the fellowship of one with the shepherd is likened to the cluster of henna. Henna was thought to be much like cypress. Henna was characteristically known for strong aromas. Be not deceived. Our thoughts, actions, and fruit yield an aroma. For example, the prayers of the saints are "as sweet smelling incense to the Lord." (Psalm 141:2) Sin, on the other hand, is disgusting to Him.

What fragrance are we letting off? Are we bragging about being outwardly dressed in our own sight impeccably only to find out that according to Scriptural principles we are so far from putting on Jesus (Galatians 3:27, Ephesians 4:22-31, Colossians3:8-14, Hebrews 2:5-13) Are we dressed in church religious doctrines, man-made rules, and behaviors that have not resulted in a commensurate change in attitude?

Only by abiding in the shepherd, Jesus Christ Himself, can our bosoms be filled with the depth of holiness, righteousness, and integrity. It is no mistake that the henna flower is the one used here to represent the sweet fellowship with our Creator. Of all flowers the flowers of the henna plant are more tightly clustered that any other flowers in Israel. We must allow the Holy Spirit to search and probe our innermost being (Psalm 139) that we can develop into believers who are intimately tightly clustered around our shepherd. What would this look like?

This one's garments are "washed in wine" and his clothes are "dripping in the blood of grapes" (Genesis 49:11)

Like many today Isaiah asks of the Lord why"[His] apparel is splashed in red and [His] garments like the one who treads in the winepress." The Lord's answer is similar to that which the Holy Spirit still speaks today- "I have trodden the winepress alone and there were none with me...I stained all my rainment...I looked but...there was no one to uphold my truth." (Isaiah 63:5).If the Lord finds anything other than things which line up within His holiness and righteousness there will be gleaning. There "will be no singing, nor is there joyful sound; the treaders tred no wine in the press; for the shout of joy has been made to cease." (Isaiah 16:10).

What will the Lord see when He searches today for the choice grapes? Will He only see a small remnant group who is scattered? Will He find many faithful? Or will it be as Isaiah 24:6-14 states:

Therefore hath the curse devoured the earth, and they that dwell therein are desolate: therefore the inhabitants of the earth are burned, and few men left. The new wine mourns, the vine languishes, all the merryhearted sigh. The mirth of tabrets ceases, the noise of them that rejoice ends, the joy of the harp ceases. They shall not drink wine with a song; strong drink shall be bitter to them that drink it. The city of confusion is broken down: every house is shut up, that no man may come in. There is a crying for wine in the streets; all joy is darkened, the mirth of the land is gone. In the city is left desolation, and the gate is smitten with destruction. When thus it shall be in the midst of the land among the people, there shall be as the shaking of an olive tree, and as the gleaning grapes when the vintage is done. They shall lift up their voice, they shall sing for the majesty of the LORD, they shall cry aloud from the sea.

Gleaning was the process whereby the poor came by and collected what they could that had dropped down from the harvest that remained on the ground. The Lord's desire was never for His people to just glean. That is why the Israelites were so miserable when they tried to collect up the bits of manna. The Lord always has a much better plan for His own. Abiding in the cluster and being tightly knit to Him should result in the knowledge that God will never leave the [uncompromisingly] righteous forsaken or their seed begging bread." (Psalm 37:25)

The choice is yours. God will never make the choice for you. He already has proven Himself faithful. Today can be your resurrection day or you can continue living each day of your life in emotional death and stuckness. Today can start a new perspective for you even if your circumstances do not change.

Appropriating God's Attributes

O ne of the Psalms which is of great encouragement is Psalm 27:

> The Lord is my light and my salvation; whom shall I fear? The Lord is the strength of my life; of whom shall I be afraid? When the wicked, even mine enemies and my foes, came upon me to eat up my flesh, they stumbled and fell. Though a host should encamp against me, my heart shall not fear: though war should rise against me, in this will I be confident ... For in the time of trouble He shall hide me in His pavilion n: in the secret of His tabernacle shall He hide me; He shall set me up upon a rock.

There are many names for God. Why does what name we call Him matter? The name you call something determines what you think about that thing, issue, person, circumstance. Recall earlier when we talked about the power of both thoughts and words. What we state, believe, and declare determines our victory or lack thereof over helplessness and hopelessness. For example, if you are in emotional pain it is easy to not want to state positives about people and places around us, about our own lives, or about God. It becomes more natural and habitual at times to see everything on global, absolute negative terms.

A name describes the type of relationship and function of something. Did you know that there are hundreds of Bible verses and examples both in Scripture and in people's lives today of how the names of God can work?

You may be tempted to think things like "He may be a help or a savior but not a healer" or "He may be a deliverer for Daniel in the lion's den or Joseph when his brothers turned their backs on him but /he is not a deliver, helper, or friend for me. When you realize the importance of names I believe you will be just as blessed as I am y this awareness. Once you know more about the names of God you can appropriate the meaning of these names to what you need God to be for you. Do you need a healer, a present help, a friend, a provider, some peace, someone to wait through things of life with you? I am quite certain that whatever the narrative of what had led you to this pace now you will find something reassuring in the names of God.

Who is God?

The first name we will look at is *God as deliverer*. In Psalms 62:6 God is called a fortress, deliverer, and a shield. Sometimes you are tired in life of feeling as if the "fiery darts" (see Ephesians 6:13-17) of life keep coming one after another. But He is a fortress. You can hide behind him. Since He had the victory of the resurrection on Calvary He can also be a shield that all your troubles, trials, and stresses must pass through. If something is besetting you it has to pass through Him. He has to have grace for you to handle it. He has to have an answer that you may not have yet considered. He has to see you succeeding and overcoming in and through Him.

For this reason the psalmist David says "I shall not be shaken." (Psalm 46:1-3) Have you ever felt shaken? We all have at one time or another. What if even though the winds and storms of life and blowing in many directions we are able to hide in the stability of God?

Another awesome thing about God being our rescue and help is that He is not just any old help. The Bible says in 2 Samuel 22:2 He is "a very present help in time of trouble." Those are some powerful words which stress and emphasize the type of help He is. I think of when an appliance needs repaired and a fix- it person needs called. For example, we recently had to call during one of the hottest seasons of the summer for someone to replace a motor on the air conditioning unit. In our natural lives the fix-it person seems to take forever to schedule a day to come to fix things. Then it appears as if he takes a while to do the job. He may have to return several times to pin-point the precise nature of the problem. God is different that way. He "knows your thoughts from afar" (Psalm 139:2). He knows "the number of hairs on your head." (Luke 12:7) He knew from the times you were being "knit in your mother's womb" (Jeremiah 1:5) that you would go through what you are going through now. The good news is that this also means that He knows your answer. He is eager to help. He is not bothered by your asking. The situation may not immediately change in the way you want but I can assure you based on God's character being consistent and reliable and true to His promises that He is only waiting for you to ask Him.

Sometimes the problem is that we ask everyone else instead of God. On the other hand we may consider God's take as just one option after talking with several friends and trying all our own resources. We don't consider Him a ready, quick, powerful and able help. We consider gossiping and telling our story to all the relatives, neighbors, and coworkers a better option than going to God- only to later find out we are still troubled.

Another name of God is *Sovereign*. He is in charge of everything. Not only is He concerned about what concerns us in a personal way as we just saw but He is also majestic and holy. Psalm 135:6 and Psalm 115:3 tells us that God rules over the heavens and earth, seas, and land. It says, "He does what He pleases." We have a God who nature, health problems, financial stresses, relational issues, personal wounds, and all sorts of things have to bow to.

You can either look at this as "the great, majestic God controls it all. I don't stand a chance!" or you can look at it as a personal God who cares intimately and desires to help wanting to do what's best for you. Remember He breathed life into dust and shaped and molded miraculously the miracle of you. He is called the Potter and He knows how to keep molding and shaping things if you will allow Him to. While He is sovereign He is also a gentleman and will not force Himself on anyone. If you still think you can do a better job at molding your life even though your ways haven't lessened the depression so far He won't stop you. He won't force Himself on you. He will wait and hope and long for His strength to be made perfect in your weak efforts.

What if today you and I would allow Him to mold our lives as He wills? Let's face it. We don't often do such a great job of it ourselves. Romans 9:19-21 reminds us:

> Thou wilt say then unto me, Why does he yet find fault? For who hath resisted his will? But, O man, who art thou that replies against God? Shall the

thing formed say to him that formed it, Why hast you made me thus? Hath not the potter power over the clay, of the same lump to make one vessel unto honor, and another unto dishonor?

God's sovereignty can be a real comfort to you and I in trouble if we will allow the name of Sovereign God to minster to us. For example, the fact that He is sovereign means that "nothing will be impossible with God." (Luke 1:37) We can say with our heads lifted high to heaven and with utmost confidence, "I know that You can do all things and no purpose of Yours can be thwarted." (Job 42:2)

Did you realize that the person in the Bible who that last quote is from, Job, is a person who had boils on his body, whose wife mocked and left him, whose livelihood in farming and cattle were all ruined? Even when he had reason and opportunity to "curse God and die" (Job 2:9) as the voice of the devil and flesh reminded him He chose to look to his sovereign God. In case you do not know the ending of the Job story I will share it with you. People had to eat their words after they mocked him. His religious friends who blamed him for his troubles had to see that God found him honorable and it wasn't because of some deep, dark sin that trouble beset him. Though his wife turned on him, his children died, and his livelihood was lost at first, far more was restored in the long run.

We don't know the end of the story. We may not have all the specifics which undoubtedly can be mighty frustrating. We know, however, according to Scripture that God looks to see who strives to walk uprightly before him. "Those who contend with the Lord will be shattered. Against them He will thunder in the heavens, The Lord will judge the ends of the earth; And He will give strength to His king, And will exalt the horn of His anointed." (1

Samuel 2:10) If you have been relying on His strength His ability and power can work through you to eventually manifest "abundantly beyond all you ask or think."

God loves to show off. He is no different in this way from a good earthly parent. He loves to help, assist, listen to, and be available for his earthly children. He loves to see us go from the mess we once were to the miracles we can be in Him. Though it meant brutal suffering "for the joy set before Him He endured the cross, despising the shame, and has sat down at the right hand of the throne of God." (Hebrews 12:2) What is joyous about having your skin ripped? What is joyous about the emotional mockery of which He was made? What is joyous about the betrayal and hurt by the every crowds He gave food to, cured, provided hope for, and reached out to in so many ways?

Any of us who is a parent knows there is a joy in being willing to sacrifice to do just about anything for your child. It is joyous for a parent to be available for their child because in their heart they only thrive on wanting the best for their child regardless of the pain and discomfort it may be to them. Perhaps you know this only too well. Your natural child may be stubborn and strong-willed. He or she may have an attitude and forsake the values you instilled in him or her.

We can be humbled knowing that it is a miracle for God to write such amazing stories in such foolish vessels as all of us. This is what Elijah witnessed. Even though he was one of God's chosen mouthpieces to the people, when he came in contact with a sovereign God he realized how small, feeble, and incapable on his own he is. Upon coming into contact with the sovereignty and majesty of God Elijah states, "Woe is me, for I am ruined! Because I am a man of unclean lips, And I live among a people of unclean lips; For my eyes have seen the King, the LORD of hosts." (Isaiah 6:5) This can likewise be our response to our Sovereign God today who is a king over all you go through. We can say in our hearts and proclaim aloud, "Who would not fear You, O King of the nations? Indeed it is Your due! For among all the wise men of the nations and in all their kingdoms, there is none like You." (Jeremiah 10:7)

The most magnificent thing is that this wonderfully amazing God chooses to dwell in us people. He chooses to help, assist, walk alongside, save, deliver, rescue, and be available for "temples not made by human hands." (Acts 17:24) "We have such a high priest, who has taken His seat at the right hand of the throne of the Majesty in the heavens." (Hebrews 8:1) This is our Sovereign God. This is the name *El Elyon* in Hebrew. May He reign more than our own perceptions and our own misunderstanding about the pain we are going through now.

Not only is God a helper, friend, and sovereign but He also is called *El Roi*. This name means the God who sees. You may be wondering if anyone sees or cares about your suffering. But all the while God is looking upon you. Psalm 94:9 puts it an interesting way: "He that planted the ear, shall He not hear? He that formed the eye, shall he not see?" I have had to trust this in my own life. There are people who have maintained lies against me which pain me every day of my life and refuse to come can and tell the truth. Don't you think it is hard to look at certain people when you have to regularly interact with them yet they have lied on you, been abusive, and backstabbed you? You are not alone. I have situational concerns which I wait upon the Lord God about. I don't know if certain people who have hurt me the most will ever tell the truth about what they have done and will ever apologize. I don't know if certain deep seated desires and prayers I have regarding certain hopes will ever come to pass the way I want them. I do not know how many situations will be handled. But I know that my God in the heavens see all. Those who have lied on me and done things against me will have to answer to God. For every day I have had to endure much pain and every prayer and tears I have cried in secret God who sees has a response and will hold all of us accountable. God sees every ache, pain, heartbreak, and manipulation. Everything I have and will go through God sees.

The same is true for your life for God is no respected of persons. Please don't believe that lie that "if God really saw He should have done ____." God surely has ways far beyond our ways. What you have endured may have bene more painful than anything you could have imagined. What someone said to you may have cut to the core of your heart. The actions people did may have rocked your world to where you do not even believe you have energy and ability to trust again. Allow the darkest moments in your life to be tools in the hands of a god who does not simply overlook your pain but wants to give you a perfect outcome in His way, His time, and with His justice and mercy.

If I did not believe God sees I would have long given up. When situations don't change at our pace we sometimes feel like giving up. When people don't acknowledge their horrible abuses and lies and underhandedness towards us, God sees. When we have endured in many tears God sees.

David's psalms suggest that he was someone who wept bitterly as he felt on many occasions as if His enemies were prevailing. For example, in Psalms 6:6 David says, "I am worn out from groaning; all night long I flood my bed with weeping and drench my couch with tears."

He asserts an active command for evil to flee saying in Psalms 6:8 "away from me, all you who do evil, for the Lord has heard my weeping." Finally, David acknowledges and rejoices in God's ability to turn around "my wailing into dancing; you removed my sackcloth and clothed me with joy." (Psalms 30:11)

David did not cry one or two tears. He drenched his pillow. He saturated it with tears. He has a depth of pain like me and you. He makes it clear that was it not for God he would have given up. If He did not believe God sees He could not have gone on. Imagine a wicked king Saul actively and seemingly continuously plotting against your life. You have to be around this man frequently yet when you have the opportunity to do him in you allow the God who sees to do it in his way and time.

This may be the case in your life. You probably feel as I have felt that it would be easier if you did not have to see certain people or interact with them. It would be a lot smoother of a situation if God could just relocate the people, places and things which are stressors to some other place. However, this usually is not what happens. In order to experience the complete victory God often allows us to walk past the stressors in our lives while applying what we know about Him.

Do you and I believe that the God who sees will help us through situations even when the other person never apologizes? Do we believe that God is more concerned about maturing our reactions to abuses, pains, and emotional wounds? Do we believe that God aches to see us lacking sleep, not eating, and suffering because of preoccupation with things? Ultimately do we trust the secret depths of our heart crying out to God when others have not proved trustworthy?

The same is true for your life for God is no respected of persons. Please don't believe that lie that "if God really saw He should have done ____." God surely has ways far beyond our ways. What you have endured may have bene more painful than anything you could have imagined. What someone said to you may have cut to the core of your heart. The actions people did may have rocked your world to where you do not even believe you have energy and ability to trust again. Allow the darkest moments in your life to be tools in the hands of a god who does not simply overlook your pain but wants to give you a perfect outcome in His way, His time, and with His justice and mercy.

God sees. Because our God is just He does not just see what others have done to me. He sees the thoughts and intents of my heart. Because He sees He can search and probe the depths of my heart daily and show me His truthful assessment of what He says about me. What if you and I agreed to just surrender our perceptions about ourselves, our lives, and others to God? It might look like praying Psalm 139:

O Lord, thou hast searched me, and known me. You know my downsitting and my uprising, you understand my thoughts afar off. You compass my path and my lying down, and art acquainted with all my ways. For there is not a word in my tongue, but, lo, O Lord, thou know it altogether. Thou hast beset me behind and before, and laid thine hand upon me. Such knowledge is too wonderful for me; it is high, I cannot attain unto it. Whither shall I go from thy spirit? or whither shall I flee from thy presence? If I ascend up into heaven, thou art there: if I make my bed in hell, behold, thou art there. If I take the wings of the morning, and dwell in the uttermost parts of the sea; Even there shall thy hand lead me, and thy right hand shall hold me. If I say, Surely the darkness shall cover me; even the night shall be light about me. Yea, the darkness hides not from thee; but the night shines as the day: the darkness and the light are both alike to thee. For thou hast possessed my reins: thou hast covered me in my mother's womb. I will praise thee; for I am fearfully and wonderfully made: marvellous are thy works; and that my soul knows right well. My substance was not hid from thee, when I was made in secret, and curiously wrought in the lowest parts of the earth. Thine eyes did see my substance, yet being unperfect; and in thy book all my members were written, which in continuance were fashioned, when as yet there was none of them. How precious also are thy thoughts unto me, O God! how great is the sum of them! If I should count them, they are more in number than the sand: when I awake, I am still with thee. Surely thou wilt slay the wicked, O God: depart from me therefore, ye bloody men. For they speak against thee wickedly, and thine enemies take thy name in vain. Do not I hate them, O Lord, that hate thee? and am not I grieved with those that rise up against thee? I hate them with perfect hatred: I count them mine enemies. Search me, O God, and know my heart: try me, and know my thoughts: And see if there be any wicked way in me, and lead me in the way everlasting.

You may be suffering in silence but I assure you God sees. You may have aches and pains you think people barely know about but God sees. You may have so many layers of life's hurts piled up that you think there is no way to untangle theme but God sees. Man looks outwardly but God's truth is all that really matters. No one is tricking God at all. There may be a pastor on the pulpit who charismatically teaches something but is far from the Lord in His own heart. The Lord sees. There may be a person pretending to be something outwardly who has been hurtful, manipulative and underhanded in ways that are not seen in the open but God sees. God will look upon our hearts with truthfulness now but will in the end render a just and perfect judgment. The Lord Himself speaks in Jeremiah

17:9-10, "I the Lord search the heart, I try the reins, even to give every man according to his ways, and according to the fruit of his doings."

Just like David you may have had many a time where you wanted to give up. We have to actively remind ourselves that the Lord sees and hears. He is attentive when we call to Him and nothing passes Him by. "The eyes of the Lord are toward the righteous, and His ears are open to their cry." (Psalm 34:15)

Nothing is hidden from our all-seeing God. He does not get mad when we speak before Him with honest concern. He hears your grief, helplessness, anger, and gut wrenching pain. God is not in denial about the depth of the hurt. This is why sometimes it is good to beseech God for help.

Recall Psalm 139 listed earlier above. This psalm can serve as a role model for us. David asks for help in three areas. These three areas are places we, too, can receive help from the all-seeing God:

1. He ask for God to show him his own thoughts even in the midst of the pain that he may think soberly and holy while grieving his enemies
2. He asks God to search his behavior to see if there be any wicked response.
3. He asks God to lead him as he acknowledges that his own responses, because of the depth of hurt and pain he feels, would not be pretty.

To me, however, one of the best parts of this psalm is when He states "thou has possessed my reins." That is hard to say in the pain. God, I trust that you see. I don't want to handle the reins of my life anymore.

This goes back to what we said earlier in the book about casting our cares on the more experienced one- God. His timing, his answers may not be as we would have it. In fact, often they are not. It is a matter of reminding ourselves of the fact that not only does God see but He sees perfectly. Nothing gets past him. Perhaps your child has lied and manipulated but your spouse does not see and know it all. God sees. Perhaps your co-workers seem to be getting ahead while walking dishonestly yet you lag behind while acting uprightly. God sees. Perhaps the person who hurt you the most appears to be going on and living the good life while you ache and pain but God sees. Perhaps your body aches with little relief but God sees.

If He sees He will respond. It is all about if we will allow Him to possess the reins. This is what the answer for depression, discouragement, hopelessness, suicide is about. Zechariah 4:10 asks, "Who hath despised the day of small things? For they shall rejoice... the eyes of the LORD, run to and fro through the whole earth". Again we hear in 1 Peter 3:13 that "the eyes of the Lord are over the righteous, and His ears are open unto their prayers: but the face of the Lord is against them that do evil."

One day I was beyond myself emotionally about those who has continued to lie and not tell the truth. I cried and prayed in a closed, locked room for two days. I drenched my pillow. Then finally out of exhaustion I fell asleep and God made His word come alive to me clearly. I had a dream where God showed me the fullness of the Scripture: "neither is there any creature that is not manifest in his sight: but all things are naked and opened unto the eyes of him with whom we have to do." (Hebrews 4:13)

"This goes back to what we said earlier in the book about casting our cares on the more experienced one- God. His timing, his answers may not be as we would have it. In fact, often they are not. It is a matter of reminding ourselves of the fact that not only does God see but He sees perfectly. Nothing gets past him.

God wants to do the same for you in your situation now. Every creation is manifest to Him. There is no hiding. There are no excuses.

What is God looking for most when He sees? He is not looking for who has been through the worst or best in life. He is looking for those who turn to him whatever aches, pains, and cares they have. The Bible tells us that "the Lord looked down from heaven upon the children of men, to see if there were any that did understand, and seek God." (Psalm 14:2, Psalm 53:2)

God is watching us. "The eyes of the Lord are surely on those who fear him" (Psalm 33:18) "and on the righteous." (Psalm 34:15, 1 Peter 3;12) He is a people watcher. (Job 7:20) Anything and everything you and I think is in secret is not to Him for we are told in Scripture "your Father sees in secret." (Matthew 6:4)

We continue to see that God's names and functions are endless. He is also our *Jehovah Ezer*, the Lord our Helper. Let's face it. We think erroneously that we know what kind of help we need yet if we really knew we would have gotten ourselves out of this present mess a long time ago. It is only in the name of Jehovah-Ezer, our Helper, that we are "set securely on high." (Psalm 20:1)

One of the biggest problems people have is fearing other people. The Bible talks about this fear of man thing. You and I can set ourselves up for pain when we give so much power to someone else to make us or break us when really they do not have that power. Hebrews 13:5-6 asks, "what shall man do to me?" Maybe it is about time that we ask and answer that question Biblically. Do we believe "if God is for us who can be against us?" (Romans 8:31) I have had to hold onto that daily when people's behavior around me does not change and they go on hiding the truth and not humbly apologizing or admitting the terrible pain they've caused. I have to by God's grace continue loving those whose hearts which are so unlovely and stubborn are hardened and cold. I have to do this because God is my Jehovah Ezer, my Helper.

How can our hearts succumb to despair when we have learned that the one who is Helper is so powerful and majestic? I don't know of any counselor, master, doctor, lawyer, or assistant who can say that! When Scripture refers to God as Healer it uses the word *boethos*. What we are supposed to be doing is found in the word *boethos*. We are supposed to be crying out and running to – "bo" our God –"theos." We are supposed to cry out of the depths of our heart to Him. I remember, for example, a health issue that was plaguing me. I was bleeding incessantly and even with mega doses of hormones the bleeding would not stop. Finally, I went into the secret place alone with God in prayer and having a heart to heart talk. I cried my eyes out and my heart cried out. I can remember like it was yesterday saying "Lord, if you don't heal me I won't be healed." There is nothing any medicine or doctor can do.

By then I had episodes on many occasions of bleeding where I became extremely weak. I prayed many a time but this time there was a distinct separation from everything and throwing myself on God. "If you don't do it, I won't be healed," I cried out. And in a short time after that the healing manifested. Dr. Jesus heard my running to Him.

It is not always the first time you or I ask that we see the miracle manifest. There is a Scripture that says, "ask and you shall receive; seek, and you shall find; knock and it shall be opened." (Matthew 7:7-12). The original words here mean knock and ask with a persistence of knowing that the Sovereign God who sees and delivers is on the job. Knock and ask perfectly with a thankful heart each time even when the result does not seem manifest for years. Know and ask like it is done as soon as you ask Him and you will see it eventually!

God doesn't just help in a general sense but He desires to provide and lead us to provision. To this end He is called our *Jehovah Jireh*, our provider. The problem is we get caught up in so many erroneous ways of thinking about God's providing being dong exactly what we want or desire in the way we demand it. False preachers have deluded so many that if you just say it in Jesus' name He has to do it. But what they do not teach is that what is being prayed, quoted, said, and desired must be consistent with Scriptural principles, consistent with the fact of who God is and for our well being and His glory.

Philippians 4:19 states that "my God will supply every need of yours according to his riches in glory in Christ Jesus." We forget, however, that not everything we want is a genuine need. We do not need a big car. We do not need excessive worldly extravagance. We need "our daily bread." (Matthew 6:11) We need the daily sustenance to get by. To this end God will help you be able to obtain and hold a job or persevere at a task. Be faithful at what is set for you. He will grace you to pay the basic bills and have groceries for your needs.

The Psalmist states that he "has never seen the righteous forsaken or His seed begging bread." (Psalm 37:25) Keep in mind these names of God are for "the righteous to implement. We cannot do any old thing we please however we want and then get angry when God is not a magic genie providing the means we want in the way we want.

We must understand what this Scripture means then. It means He will not leave us destitute if we walk by His strength and grace uprightly before Him. He can use ways we cannot even imagine when we know him to reach to our needs. Perhaps he can put on heart of someone a need and they suddenly drop food or a bag of groceries by your house. Maybe a neighbor brings by some leftovers even though they did not know your situation of food dwindling. Maybe a church member helps assist with your household and kids while you are having to attend to certain things. Maybe someone says "a word in due season" (aka- at the appropriate time- Proverbs 25:11) not even knowing exactly what you are going through but that word provides the exact wisdom and direction you need. That's our amazing God in action.

Another name of our amazing, sensitive, caring, personal and majestic God is *Jehovah Rapha*. The name *Jehovah-Rapha* is a name that speaks to us and our need today. We live in a stressful world and society. Every day new problems confront us as we bend under the load of seemingly unsolvable problems. In spite of burdens sometimes one mile high which weigh heavy on someone's chest we have assurance that if we trust in Him, He is faithful to deliver. This is His promise, over and over again.

Healing embodies both the physical and emotional. Notice in Jeremiah 30:17 that God promises "I will restore you to health and heal your wounds." That "and" is important. He cares intimately about your physical ability to do the day to day tasks as well as our emotional wherewithal to handle stresses. Isaiah 40:18-29 promises us that "He will not grow tired or weary, and his understanding no one can fathom. He gives strength to the weary and increases the power of the weak." Even when the pain seems so extreme as in Job's situation in which He lost everything we ca say "This would be my comfort; I would even exult in pain unsparing, for I have not denied the words of the Holy One, my God." (Job 6:10)

God has several "tactics" He uses:

1. **He bears our pain**. He didn't go to Calvary for nothing. He took on every pain, sin and depravity, mistake, wrong decision, sickness, wound and issue you and everyone else has. Then He resurrected with a marvelous victory. He did not take it on so you could take it on again and again and play junior savior. "Surely he has taken up our grief and pain, and carried our sorrows. He carried our grief, sorrow and pain on Calvary." (Isiah 53:3-4)

2. **God leads you with His wisdom in your situation**. As the more experienced one to which you are yoked He lifts you up and ploughs the land of the wilderness and stress you are in. Don't drag Him along with you as if you are the more experienced one for this can never work. What can any of us tell our majestic God? Why not allow God's strong hand and ability to be a better leader and conqueror than we are guide us perfectly? (see 1 Peter 5:6-7)

3. **God allows us to wait and rest while he is doing things behind the scenes**. We forget that just because results have not manifest or are not yet seen with our narrow tunnel vision does not mean God did not hear your heart's cry at the very first moment. Waiting upon Him will never disappoint. Isaiah 40:31 promises us that:

But they that wait upon the LORD shall renew their strength; they shall mount up with wings as eagles; they shall run, and not be weary; and they shall walk, and not faint.

4. **God will allow us to feel our own insufficiency that we may appreciate His all sufficiency**. Scripture states that "weeping may tarry for the night, but joy comes with the morning."(Psalm 30:5) Across a lifetime there is only God's love. The nights of crying your eyes out will give way to days of laughter. "The Lord is near to the brokenhearted and saves the crushed in spirit. If your heart is broken, you'll find God right there; If the wind is knocked out of you, he'll help you catch your breath." (Psalm 34:18) The "wind" here refers to your spirit. This verse is saying that if your spirit has no strength left and someone or something has crushed it so much that you are utterly downtrodden He will be near and will be your breath and strength. His spirit will seemingly out of nowhere strengthen you.

5. **The Lord allows time to pass that the fullness of His glory might be revealed in a situation when His solution comes**. Remember when Lazarus, his friend, was dead and the sister was so stressed? (John 11:38-44) Jesus could have panicked like most of us and run to raise him from the dead but He waited that there may be no doubt of foul play, no temptation of any other explanation but for God's glory to be revealed. Jesus was never in a hurry to do things out of anxious panic. Even when his mother asked that He do a miracle and provide drink for those at the wedding at Cana, Jesus cautioned her about doing things too quickly. (John 2:1-11) Do we just want a quick answer to our pain or do we want "a whole, complete and perfect work" of God for His glory to be done? (James 1:4) Brother Paul puts things in a

beautiful eternal perspective when he says, "For I consider that the sufferings of this present time are not worth comparing with the glory that is to be revealed to us."(Romans 8:18) God is telling us that there is no comparison between the present hard times and the coming good times when we are forever with the Lord.

6. **God wants us to know true peace- not peace of circumstances always changing immediately as we desire but peace of a relationship with Him who is peace**. He speaks the same to us as He did to the disciples: "Peace I leave with you; my peace I give you. I do not give to you as the world gives. Do not let your hearts be troubled and do not be afraid. Peace. I don't leave you the way you're used to being left—feeling abandoned, bereft. So don't be upset. Don't be distraught." (John 14:7)

God's names are truly marvellous. If we wait and rest in His character and names we can declare like the psalmist in Psalm 71:20-21:

Thou, which hast shewed me great and sore troubles, shalt quicken me again, and shalt bring me up again from the depths of the earth. Thou shalt increase my greatness, and comfort me on every side. I will also praise thee with the psaltery, even thy truth, O my God: unto thee will I sing with the harp, O thou Holy One of Israel. My lips shall greatly rejoice when I sing unto thee; and my soul, which thou hast redeemed. My tongue also shall talk of thy righteousness all the day long: for they are confounded, for they are brought unto shame that seek my hurt.

With our God in Jesus Christ through the power of the Holy Spirit we can proudly declare Psalm 73:23-28:

Thou hast held me by my right hand. Thou shalt guide me with thy counsel, and afterward receive me to glory. Whom have I in heaven but thee? and there is none upon earth that I desire beside thee. My flesh and my heart fail: but God is the strength of my heart, and my portion forever. For, lo, they that are far from thee shall perish...But it is good for me to draw near to God: I have put my trust in the Lord GOD, that I may declare all thy works.

God's names and His character are truly marvelous yet personal, lofty yet sensitive, fearless in leading yet humbly guiding us in bearing the yoke of the present concerns. When we proclaim to be believers in Christ our whole lives become about God's name. We start by acknowledging Him as Master, Owner, and Savior over our lives. Salvation is only found through and in His name (John 1:12). To His name whether now willingly or someday by force all of heaven and earth, every person, creature, demon, and power and principality will yield. "At the name of Jesus that every knee will one day bow and every tongue confess that Jesus Christ is Lord" (Phil. 2:10-11). Our prayers and petitions are to be made in His name (John 14:13-14). All we live for and go through including suffering and the place of our darkest hour must first pass through the name of God in Jesus Christ.

Prayer of Surrender

Lord, I come before you giving my feeble self as a sacrifice to you. All I have to offer you is this pained, hurting, wounded and distraught self. All I have to offer you are my methods for dealing with life that never work, at least not for very long. All I have to offer you is everything I am- weak, incapable, and powerless. I come to you trusting and declaring that you are who you say you are. You are a victor over sin, death and troubles, temptations, and habitual problems. You are not just a victor but I declare and believe now that you are my Victor. You are my present help in this very need I have. You are my healer, helper, provider, defender. You are the sovereign king over my fallen kingdom which has crushed around me. You are the builder and sustainer of all that is genuine abundant life. I choose you.

I choose you over clinging to pain. I choose you over unforgiveness and offense. I choose you over fear of people or the unknown. I choose you undoubtedly and unflinchingly. I decide that this day forward I will allow myself to be yoked to you for you are the much stronger and entirely capable experienced overcomer. Wherever you take me and whatever it looks like is okay with me even into the unknown for you are my constant and stability. Just like your crucifixion seemed to be your darkest hour yet produced great glory I invite you fully and wholly into what now feels like my darkest hour.

Lord of the dark hour you are light. I believe your light, your life, your name, and your character always dispel the negative influence of all darkness. I choose to celebrate you instead of exalting problems and pain. I celebrate what I do not see and understand. Thank you for not leaving me alone and forsaken. Thank you for clinging to me in this present time and embracing me with your sensitive heart. Thank you for gently redirecting and empathically seeing and holding every area of mine dear and precious to you. I love you Lord. I believe that the best place for this dark time is in your hands, not mine. So I'm handing it over now. May your strength be made perfect in my weakness and may your name be glorified.

Strengthen my feet for the steps ahead. Enable me to read and be guided by the Bible and the Holy Spirit in every moment. Equip me to shut out influences of people and things which are not consistent with you. Order my steps and I with walk with you, the Author and Finisher of my faith. I choose now to begin my resurrection day. I chose now for you to begin the process of renewing my mind, changing my speech and behaviors, and having a fresh outlook on things which have tried to keep me stuck. You are my perspective. I agree with you now in spite of what I may feel that if you say I am more than a conqueror through you then I am. I pick up my mat and head to the pool of your living water that you may stir your healing in my life. I allow you to destroy my mat that I have been sitting on and wallowing in this pain. Lead me to wherever you desire. I am yours. I am not destroyed, stuck, defeated, paralyzed, helpless, suicidal, homicidal, bound, orphaned, utterly alone, and forgotten. I am not ill, riddled with infirmity, and plagued with disease forever. I am yours.

In Jesus' name I pray.
Your child,

_____

(insert your name here)

Also available by Michele D. Aluoch:

Sanctuary: A Shelter For Your Soul.
(2003) Morris Publishing.

This book available directly through River of Life Professional Counseling LLC contains here and now applications of Bible verses for stress, anxiety, and other life concerns. After reading Scriptures readers are taken through imagery connected with the Scripture which helps them place themselves in Scriptures as personal and applicable in their present situations. The book has bene used in retreats, counseling sessions, private devotions, grief groups, personal reading, and other venues.

To inquire about obtaining copies of this book or about any of the other resources available through River of Life Professional Counseling LLC contact:

Michele Aluoch
River of Life Professional Counseling LLC
Website: www.rolpc.org
E mail: counselormichele@rolpc.org
Phone: (614) 353-4157

Services Available by Michele Aluoch:

- Speaking engagements
- Retreats
- Seminars
- Consultation and training for Clinical Counselors, Minsters, and Lay Persons Working with those who need emotional healing
- Clinical counseling
- Continuing education courses for mental health professionals
- Pastoral Counseling
- Pre-Marital and Marital Assessment and Consultation
- Weddings
- Prayer and Mentoring For Emotional Healing

<u>Contact</u>:
Michele Aluoch
River of Life Professional Counseling LLC
Website: www.rolpc.org
E mail: counselormichele@rolpc.org
Phone: (614) 353-4157

CPSIA information can be obtained
at www.ICGtesting.com
Printed in the USA
FFOW02n1803190615
14426FF